To ⊏

With warm wishes !

Didier

Lausanne, June 2016

Inspiring Stewardship

Inspiring Stewardship

Didier Cossin
Ong Boon Hwee

WILEY

Registered office
John Wiley & Sons Ltd, The Atrium, Southern Gate, Chichester, West Sussex, PO19 8SQ,
United Kingdom

For details of our global editorial offices, for customer services and for information about
how to apply for permission to reuse the copyright material in this book please visit our
website at www.wiley.com.

Library of Congress Cataloging-in-Publication Data

Names: Cossin, Didier, author. | Hwee, Ong Boon, 1956- author.
Title: Inspiring stewardship / Didier Cossin, Ong Boon Hwee.
Description: Hoboken : Wiley, 2016. | Includes index.
Identifiers: LCCN 2016014536| ISBN 9781119270805 (hbk)
Subjects: LCSH: Leadership. | Business ethics. | Social ethics. |
  Organizational behavior. | BISAC: BUSINESS & ECONOMICS / Finance.
Classification: LCC HD57.7 .C6725 2016 | DDC 658.4/09–dc23 LC record
  available at https://lccn.loc.gov/2016014536

A catalogue record for this book is available from the British Library.

ISBN 978-1-119-27080-5 (hbk) ISBN 978-1-119-29288-3 (ebk)

ISBN 978-1-119-29290-6 (ebk) ISBN 978-1-119-29291-3 (ebk)

Cover Design: Wiley
Cover Image: © ConstantinosZ/Shutterstock

Set in 11/13pt SabonLTStd by Aptara Inc., New Delhi, India
Printed in Great Britain by TJ International Ltd, Padstow, Cornwall, UK

Contents

Acknowledgments

We would like to thank the members of the Stewardship Asia Centre board: Mr Hsieh Fu Hua, Ms Chan Wai Ching, Mr Goh Yong Siang, Mr Simon Israel, Mrs Lim Hwee Hua, and Ms Jacqueline Wong for their intellectual contribution in shaping this book.

We are deeply grateful to the many steward leaders who inspired us to write this book.

Thank you to Sophie Coughlan, Martin Kralik, and Hongze (Abraham) Lu for their help in conducting the background research.

Our sincere thanks go to Stuart Crainer for his help in editing this book. We are also grateful to Manjith Manohar at the IMD Global Board Center, Tracy Lee at Temasek Management Services, and Joanna Soh at the Stewardship Asia Centre for their support.

Many thanks also to Carine Dind at IMD and Yves Balibouse, who were instrumental in the book production as well as to Susan Stehli at IMD for the final proofreading, and to George Curzon at Indexing Specialists (UK) Ltd for the index.

About the Authors

Didier Cossin, Professor & Director
IMD Global Board Center, IMD – International Institute of
Management Development, Lausanne, Switzerland
Board Member, Stewardship Asia Centre, Singapore
www.imd.org/boardcenter

Didier Cossin is a professor at IMD and the director of the IMD Global Board Center. Over the last 25 years, his research has spanned best-in-class governance practices and the build-up of successful organizations, including multinational corporations, financial institutions whether private or supranational, sovereign wealth funds, humanitarian organizations, and public administration. He is an advisor to chairmen and boards of some of the largest corporate, financial, and not-for-profit organizations across many geographies (Europe, Asia, Africa, Middle East, Americas). Professor Cossin holds a PhD from Harvard University (Robert C. Merton Chair) and is a former Fulbright Fellow at the Massachusetts Institute of Technology, Department of Economics (USA). He is a former student of ENS rue d'Ulm (France) and holds masters degrees from Sorbonne University and EHESS (France).

Before joining IMD, Didier Cossin worked for Goldman Sachs, has taught at Harvard University, and was a professor at HEC, University of Lausanne, chairing the university's Department of Management and directing its Institute of Banking & Finance.

Professor Cossin is the author and co-author of four books, a number of book chapters, and many articles which have obtained citations of excellence or other awards. He holds the UBS Chair in Banking and Finance at IMD and has also received distinctions such as the Febelfin BFI Chair and the Deloitte Risk Management Chair.

ONG Boon Hwee, Chief Executive Officer
Stewardship Asia Centre, Singapore
http://www.stewardshipasia.com.sg

Mr Ong Boon Hwee is the CEO of Stewardship Asia Centre, a Singapore-based thought leadership centre that focuses on promoting stewardship and governance of companies and organizations across Asia. He directs SAC's efforts to develop and propagate a greater understanding of stewardship, a concept that emphasizes safeguarding and enhancing an organization's ability to create economic and societal value over time.

Prior to joining Stewardship Asia Centre, Mr Ong gained experience working in the corporate as well as the public sector. He started Beyond Horizon Consulting, a Singapore-based company that focuses on leadership development and strategic planning. He was the COO of Singapore Power (SP), responsible for its Singapore operations and also corporate functions. Before that, he was a Managing Director at Temasek Holdings, responsible for Strategic Relations & Projects, and concurrently the CEO of the Temasek Management Services Group (TMS), managing subsidiaries of diverse businesses including IT, training and logistics. And in his earlier military career, Brigadier-General Ong held key command and staff positions in the Singapore Armed Forces (SAF).

Mr Ong serves as a director on the boards of a number of companies and non-profit organizations. He graduated with First Class Honors in Economics from the National University of Singapore, and holds a Masters Degree in Military Arts & Science from the United States Command & General Staff College.

Introduction

"How can a business thrive and sustain growth while enhancing the wealth of its stakeholders and the well-being of the societies in which it operates over the long term?"

The notion of stewardship has never been more relevant to business than it is today. In a world where the ownership of firms is increasingly fragmented, and investment structures are more and more complex, the time horizons of investors, executives, and owners do not always coincide. Managing competing interests to find the right balance between short- and long-term considerations is perplexing for many leaders.

Stewardship is an inspiring way to revitalize this discussion. It encourages business leaders to shift mind-sets, to creatively engage their organizations and other societal actors, and to enhance wealth creation for all.

Stewardship requires the ability to step back, to consider the full extent to which business impacts depend on the relationship among different groups of people, the context in which the business operates, and the time horizons over which business activities occur.

We define this sort of organizational stewardship as the act of safeguarding and enhancing the capability of the organization to create economic and societal value over time.[1]

Let's be clear. Economic returns are fundamental to any firm's objectives. But, beyond that, stewardship advocates actively and constantly considering the value generated for the people critical to business success. Stewardship is inclusive. It demands consideration of the full roster of value-creating actors, including:

- Customers, suppliers, employees, investors, and stakeholders; those on whom a company's success ultimately depends;

1

- The local community, society, and the environment; the people and areas directly and indirectly affected by the firm's activities;
- Future generations; taking a long-term view, which safeguards the interests of those who succeed us.

By enlarging the spheres considered as relevant to a firm's activities, and looking to a much longer-term horizon, stewardship can help businesses deliver societal and economic returns.

The Stewardship Challenge

There is no doubt that for many organizations and their leaders, stewardship presents an enormous challenge – both intellectually and practically. Until recently, the dominant view of business focus was on creating value for a firm's owners and shareholders. But, along with expanding their global footprint, today's companies are compelled to redefine their view of corporate achievement and success. In essence, the stewardship perspective is built on the concept of companies being designed to create lasting positive impacts for the markets in which they operate, society, and the environment.

Despite the obvious benefits of stewardship, the business community's understanding of it remains intuitive at best. In particular, the words "stewardship" and "stewards" are often used despite not being clearly understood. Even so, many of the issues and challenges related to the concept of stewardship have been analyzed in various forms in recent years. The lenses and terminology may vary, but the themes have many echoes of stewardship.

Jerry Porras and Jim Collins conducted one of the best known of these studies. Their 1994 bestseller *Built to Last* was the result of a six-year research project that surveyed 1000 CEOs on their perceptions of what made a company visionary. It told the stories of 18 firms.

Jim Collins further developed some of the ideas in his 2001 book, *Good to Great*. Here the concept of greatness was anchored in financial indicators: The eleven companies judged to be great were those that reported financial performance several multiples better than the market average over a sustained period. One-to-one comparisons were made between companies that had fulfilled their potential and their industry peers, which had not. A team of researchers spent five years poring over records and data points.

The years that followed were not always kind to the eleven firms heralded as great: Fannie Mae became involved in well-known home mortgage scandals; Wells Fargo was among the recipients of government aid under the 2008 Troubled Asset Relief Program (TARP); a year later, Circuit City Stores filed for bankruptcy.

Whatever greatness these firms possessed seems to have been concentrated in their pre-2001 past, with little carry-over effect for the future. In hindsight, *Built to Last* and *Good to Great* suggest that organizations are live, delicate organisms whose past performance holds little predictive power for their future prospects, as well demonstrated by Phil Rosenzweig in *The Halo Effect*.[2]

Telling Stories

Our own work is built on a belief that the language of stewardship is critical. What the companies and their leaders tell the world, the narratives they create and use when they communicate, is significant. Their choice of terms – both conscious and unconscious – reflects their view of the world, and their underlying values, beliefs, and culture. As such, the language they use reveals the degree of their stewardship orientation, and offers insights about how stewardship drives decision-making. Moreover, words and languages can be described as unchanging in that they will outlive most corporate practices and even companies. Language and narratives live on in organizations.

Let us not be naive: Words can easily be turned into misleading expressions. Defamations, misinterpretations, and untruths abound. Still, words are important indicators (together with our actions) of the beliefs and culture of organizations.

With that logic in mind, the qualitative analysis in this book is reinforced by quantitative research based on an innovative approach of content analysis. The quantitative research was conducted in two steps, as detailed in the Appendix.

The first step was a word content analysis of 1.5 million words taken from the annual reports of two groups of companies. The first group was made up of companies that were potentially well stewarded and the second group comprised companies that were potentially poorly stewarded. The full list of companies can be found in the Appendix. We examined major differences in incidences of words between these two groups of companies. A word was only considered distinct if it appeared in the sample more than 20 times; the difference between its incidence in one group as opposed to the other group likewise had to be more than 20 occurrences; lastly, this difference had to be greater than 20 percent of the word's total count (across both groups). These criteria could be described as a "20/20/20" rule. Differentiating in this way enabled us to identify significant terms that were distinctive between these two groups of companies.

The findings are fascinating: there are clear (and statistically significant) differences in word usage across companies; many of these variations reflect disparate narratives constructed around company attitudes toward stakeholders, employees, debt, time, and other dimensions related to stewardship. Full details of the word content analysis are described in the Appendix.

The second step analyzed the language used in more than 2500 annual reports from 872 companies of over $10 billion in sales over several years.[3] With the two lists of distinct words specific to the companies, we constructed an Implied Stewardship Index, which was used to compare metrics across companies, as described in the Appendix.

We used the most impactful and striking results of both of these studies to inform the concepts and examples presented throughout the book. In this way, the findings provided useful insights on various dimensions of companies' activities like the use of R&D, trends in labor considerations, use of financial leverage, and so on.

The Principles of Stewardship

Our analysis combined with a literature review and qualitative studies led us to identify three key principles underpinning stewardship:

1. Leading with impact

    Steward leaders inspire their followers, cultivating a sense of personal responsibility for the long-term well-being of the organization and the contribution it makes to society. Such leaders tend to have a transformational style of leadership – creating engagement with employees at the emotional level, placing a high level of trust in subordinates, and imparting a long-term view across the organization. Steward leaders are influential and respected due to a combination of their vision, values and integrity, their ability to understand and connect this vision with the needs of others, and their ability to deliver business results.

2. Safeguarding the future of the institution

Well-stewarded organizations are built on corporate cultures where relationships are based on trust and employees are actively engaged in achieving a meaningful, lasting corporate purpose. These employees have a long-term view of their career path within the organization, concrete ideas about the possibilities afforded by the company, and an understanding of how they can best contribute their talents and energies to create value for the company.

3. Delivering meaningful benefits to society

Well-stewarded organizations understand and build on their connection to all stakeholders, and seek to play a constructive role in delivering meaningful benefits to society. They articulate clearly, consistently, and authentically what the corporate purpose is – both internally and externally – and make sure strategy and operational processes are aligned with this purpose.

In well-stewarded organizations, profit is considered to be the reward for the firm's delivery of benefit to society, rather than its objective. Though important, profit maximization is not the only objective of business. Value creation (i.e., innovating, producing, delivering products to customers) is regarded as fundamental to the firm's purpose, and needs to be balanced with value appropriation (i.e., extracting profits).[4] Staying in touch with external and internal stakeholders' expectations of the company and actively managing the gap between their expectations and the organization's activities is required to minimize discrepancies. By understanding and actively engaging with stakeholders, the organization has an impact on society that is both positive and meaningful to its stakeholders.

The Book

Part I tackles the fundamental question: *Why Stewardship?* We start by profiling a selection of steward leaders and their organizations – from Ratan Tata to Warren Buffett. This exploration uncovers insights and principles and enables a discussion on the concepts of stewardship and a societal vision for the future.

In exploring what stewardship looks like, we studied steward leaders at work in a variety of organizations and environments –

notably in situations where a volatile and uncertain context requires clear and bold direction, at inflection points and during crises. We were especially interested in the actions steward leaders took, often sacrificing short-term profits for the benefit of long-term interest. Gleaning insights from these examples, we extrapolate key stewardship dimensions and characteristics – including values and beliefs. We also tried to understand how stewards gain their inspiration as well as the powerful ways in which they communicate their vision to others – touching people with their passion to create and contribute to something bigger and more enduring than their individual lifetimes.

Part II – *What drives stewardship?* – explores the distinctive characteristics and attributes of steward leaders. Looking across different cultural contexts, we try to understand whether there is something fundamentally different about the make-up of steward leaders, how they come to have this exceptional drive, resilience, and willingness to shoulder such great responsibility. We examine business leaders' values and beliefs, as well as the personality traits and attitudes that seem to be fundamental to the stewardship mind-set.

Part III – *Stewardship in Action* – highlights a number of situations in which stewards really shifted the course of their organizations – or even their countries. We outline actions by different steward leaders demonstrating great courage in the face of difficult situations, rising to the challenge in a manner emblematic of sustained stewardship orientation. Of course, stewardship is not without its risks. We go on to examine some of the capabilities that can deepen organizational resilience, helping organizations to stay on course. We identify the best ways of securing stewardship for the next generation.

Many of our examples come from Asia – and may well be an inspiring surprise for Western readers. But, the book uses examples from throughout the world, including Europe and North America, and draws on our global research.

With a compelling vision of what a future motivated by stewardship can look like, we seek to inspire readers to find and embark on a stewardship path for their own context. To consider your own inclination as a steward leader, complete the questionnaire at the end of Chapter 7 to build your own self-awareness around each of the elements needed. This is offered not with a view to judgment or evaluation – but rather to help each of us consider our own areas of strength and those needing development.

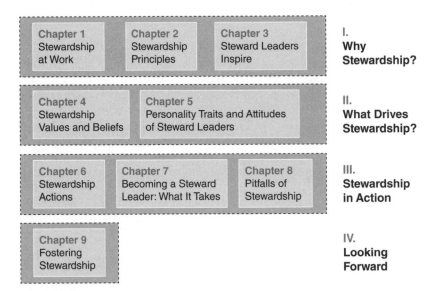

Figure I.1   Book roadmap

Stewardship offers clear financial, economic, social, and other benefits over the long term. Through this book, it is our intention to start a conversation on what stewardship looks like and the potentially game-changing contribution it can make. We encourage you to consider what impact you can make as a steward leader – individually and collectively – so that we can work together to make stewardship a reality.

The risks of not going down the stewardship path are real. Clear lines of responsibility for long-term business performance have been diluted and are in danger of dissolving. In a highly interconnected global economy, with increasingly complex and cross-boundary ownership structures, stewardship failures have real consequences – with shocks no longer contained to one context. In Part IV, we examine the forces at play that pose a real threat to global prosperity and how fostering stewardship serves to counteract these forces. Business has a key role to play in fostering a context for stewardship, in which all members of the stewardship ecosystem can contribute to creating a positive business legacy for the world and future generations.

Figure I.1 illustrates the logic of the book, providing an overview of its flow and a roadmap to guide you.

PART
I

WHY STEWARDSHIP?

Stewardship at Work

The mind-set and attributes of stewardship have been around for a long time, even if they were not always labeled as such. There are many stories of business and national leaders whose personalities and legacies have come to typify this approach. We will explore some of the situations they faced in their careers and which proved to be the catalysts of their stewardship. The color and detail of the stories give us a flavor of the type and scope of these individuals' achievements. In subsequent chapters we will examine what motivated their actions, as well as what shaped their character traits and underlying values.

It is often said that authors stand on the shoulders of giants. Our understanding of the concepts and practice of stewardship is no exception. The individuals we describe are and have been inspirations. We refer to them throughout the book to illustrate the various dimensions of stewardship, as well as to show how context shapes stewardship. The diversity of these individuals and their styles reveals the multi-dimensional nature of stewardship. We would like to stress, right at the outset, that there is no ideal individual steward, but that each of these leaders is inspirational in a particular facet of stewardship.

As we will see, these leaders emerge from very different organizational contexts including financial investors, family foundations, trans-generational family businesses, public agencies, institutional investors, and state-owned enterprises. While it may appear in different forms, depending on the nature of the organization and its environment, stewardship shares distinctive characteristics across contexts. The different contexts may influence the way in which stewardship emerges and which actors are its drivers. Generally, these actors share three key characteristics: When influence and leadership lead to clear economic benefits; when actions are driven by a long-term focus; when there is a commitment to enhance the well-being of the communities in which organizations operate impacting the societies around them – is when stewardship is at work.

The Tata Story: Blazing a Trail

The 1960s and 1970s were a time of discontent for Indian businesses. Post-independence, India was an inward-looking, command economy that, in an almost Soviet fashion, upheld the public sector at the expense of private enterprise. Those who ventured into private business had to contend with a populist government, labor problems, and a slow growth rate. Territorial conflict with neighboring countries, as well as political instability on the domestic front, meant that the Indian government declared a state of national emergency on three occasions – in 1962, 1971, and 1975, each stretching over several years.

It was in this bleak period that a young overseas graduate became involved in his family's hodgepodge of businesses, some of them dating back to the 1880s. When he joined the family company in 1962, Ratan Tata was a 25-year-old civil engineer, armed with an architecture degree from Cornell University.

Despite the restrictive business environment in India at the time, Ratan Tata instinctively focused on nurturing innovation and business excellence by setting up internal structures for collecting and evaluating new ideas. Amid a culture of lifetime employment and seniority based on age or length of service, he offered the prospect of rapid career advancement to young able managers. This gave them a sense of ownership in the company's success, and signaled a commitment to talent rather than hierarchy. Thanks to the ample space provided for professionals and intrapreneurs, the Tata business units reported consistent profitability.

As a director, Ratan Tata was tasked with growing a number of Tata enterprises in the electronics and textiles sector. His 1981 appointment as chairman of Tata Industries signaled the group's move into the advanced technology space – one of several new initiatives aimed at modernizing and transforming the company. Having set up seven subsidiaries in various high-tech segments, between

1982 and 1989 Tata Industries grew its capital and profitability tenfold.[1] Throughout this period, Ratan Tata applied himself to creating a cohesive brand for the many companies under the Tata umbrella.

Ratan Tata's clarity of purpose in pursuing not only business success but enhancing social and national economic impact was key to raising his profile, expanding his influence, and establishing him as one of India's foremost thought leaders. The discipline he had honed over many years of running a group of businesses in a challenging environment, coupled with his overseas education and exposure, also stood him in good stead. His appointment in 1991 as chairman of Tata Sons, Tata group's holding company, coincided with the tentative start of India's economic liberalization and opening the Indian markets to the rest of the world.

Even then Ratan Tata's eyes were firmly fixed on a distant horizon. He knew that with the world coming to India, the country's companies would urgently have to improve their standards. The speedy demise of the once-iconic Indian brand, the Ambassador car, once the Indian markets opened further confirmed these apprehensions.[2] Indian businesses had to learn to benchmark themselves not only against domestic players but against industry leaders from around the world; and one day, if necessary, go as far as to acquire their international competitors.[3] For the Tata group this meant reassembling an unwieldy collection of companies, some of which had competed against one another in specific segments, into a cohesive business entity with enough muscle to make its way into international markets.

The goal Ratan Tata was pursuing was far greater than creating shareholder value: it was to give India a solid base of homegrown industries. In turn, these industries would provide strong, locally branded products to the entire spectrum of India's population, across geographic, social, and economic brackets. During the 21 years of his chairmanship at Tata Sons (1991–2012), the group expanded from a medium-sized domestic focused company to a $100 billion global business, dozens of times larger in size than in 1991. Tata group became India's biggest diversified industrial group by revenue and global in terms of scale. Today, 65 percent of the company's sales come from 90 percent of its overseas markets.

"I think our contribution to the nation was in building a foundation for basic industry, creating a foundation for technology, and setting some benchmarks in corporate governance and ethical business conduct," observed Ratan Tata.[4] This illustrates his commitment to driving social good, specifically accountability, adhering to moral and ethical principles, as well as encouraging openness and transparency. His willingness to pioneer and drive these standards in Indian business is a testament to his tenacity in safeguarding the future by encouraging strong, forward-looking policies and standards.

"What I have done is establish growth mechanisms, play down individuals and play up the team that has made the companies what they are," summarized Tata.[5] He ensured rewards were distributed in a way that corresponded to contribution, rather than hierarchical power, promoting equity as a key principle. This in turn promoted the intrinsic motivation of individual employees to take ownership of Tata company objectives. Today, up-and-coming managers at Tata companies continue to be described as "true-blue Tata representatives – focused, down-to-earth and unassuming, with a deep sense of social responsibility."[6]

Ratan Tata applied high standards inside and outside the company. He was insistent that, just as companies needed to reach the highest global standards so did the Indian government. This led him to consistently reject collusion and corruption – activities often regarded as necessary in emerging markets.

He also attributed much of Tata Sons' successes to the spirit of the company's workforce, pointing out that the organization as a whole would always rise to the challenge rather than resist it.[7] To promote responsible values and provide mentoring to managers, he set up structures such as the Group Corporate Office, the members of which are recruited from senior executives from the boards of Tata companies. Their role is to act as "stewards," sharing guidance and a sense of perspective.[8]

Similarly, more than two years before Mr. Tata stepped down as chairman (on his 75th birthday in December 2012), a five-member selection committee was set up to nominate his successor. When the committee eventually put forward the name of Mr Cyrus Mistry, the departing chairman praised the move as a "good and far-sighted choice."[9] Given that more than 100 Tata companies in which the group holds mainly minority stakes are run by professional managers and independent boards, it is this understated moral guidance and a resolutely long-term view that define the group chairman's power.[10] By taking such a forward-looking and rational approach to his succession planning, Ratan Tata demonstrated prudence – effectively planning for the long term – as well as care, protecting the interests of the company in the future through continuity of leadership.

This is a notoriously difficult topic for most business leaders to discuss, and it showed Mr. Tata's commitment to the good of the collective, rather than his individual needs.

Ratan Tata is emblematic of how impactful stewardship can be in an emerging market context. His actions helped to provide a powerful footing for India – navigating the many institutional gaps that existed. His pragmatic and meritocratic business practices allowed talent to flourish, promoting significant business results for the group of companies. His concern for securing the continued success of the companies over time never wavered, as demonstrated by his role in structuring company ownership in the Tata Trusts.

Mærsk: Ownership Continuity in a Family Foundation

In 1904, A.P. Møller founded a shipping company with his father – which subsequently became Mærsk. Over the course of the next half-century, Møller grew the business, adding containers and oils to the portfolio to accelerate the company's growth. Mærsk Group is now a global conglomerate in trade, shipping, and energy. How Mærsk has flourished and ensured succession across three generations is an enlightening story.

Møller had a strong long-term focus, which he reinforced through the ownership structure of Mærsk. Three charitable foundations control the majority of shares in the Mærsk Group. This shareholding structure has been key in enabling the group to make long-term investments. While the parent company, A.P. Møller-Mærsk, is listed on the Danish Stock Exchange, the company's main shareholder is the A.P. Møller and Chastine Mc-Kinney Møller Foundation, which A.P. Møller set up in 1953 to ensure that "his life's work would always be owned by parties that held a long-term view of the company's development in the spirit of the founder and according to his principles."[11] A number of industry observers have commented on how Mærsk has never been enslaved by the obligation to deliver results for quarterly reports but rather guided by a long-time perspective and investment plan.[12]

When A.P. Møller died in 1965, his son Arnold Mærsk Mc-Kinney Møller (1913–2012) succeeded him as group chairman and

CEO. Building on strong family values, business ethics, and firm succession plans, Arnold Mærsk Mc-Kinney Møller turned the family-owned firm into a global conglomerate that includes the world's largest container shipping company, and Denmark's largest corporation, with sales of $60 billion – equivalent to nearly 20 percent of the country's GDP.[13] Mærsk Mc-Kinney Møller also sustained the long-term focus of Mærsk, with Mærsk Line investing in building double-hulled tankers that were more environmentally safe to transport oil but not making any money for the group. The belief that safe transport of oil was worth investing in and that these vessels would eventually pay off drove the decision to make short-term sacrifices for long-term growth.

Building upon his father's legacy, Mærsk Mc-Kinney Møller internalized A.P. Møller's mantra: "no loss should hit us which could be avoided with constant care" and making it core to the corporate purpose. "Constant care," alongside humbleness, uprightness, "our employees," and "our name" became recognized as the group's core values – formalized in 2003 but practiced ever since 1904.[14] Mærsk Mc-Kinney Møller took this to heart and insisted that trust was a key operating principle for the company: "The basic principle is that people can trust us. Authorities can trust us, employees can trust us and business connections can trust us. Your word should be your bond."[15]

Well into his 90s, Mærsk Mc-Kinney Møller was said to demonstrate the same degree of passion and drive for business as he did in 1940 when he first joined the company's management team. He kept a close eye on the firm's operations and had no tolerance for leadership that deviated from the family vision of Mærsk's purpose. For example, in 2007 CEO Søderberg was fired due to the mistakes made after the €2.3 billion takeover of the world's third-largest container line (at the time) P&O Nedlloyd.

The company never wavered in embracing its values and the importance of ensuring they were engrained. In transitioning from family leadership to a professional CEO – Nils S. Andersen – in 2007, the group embarked on an enormous values program involving 900 people, where the values were cascaded down into the next generation to ensure that they continued to be core to the company's purpose. At the time of publication, the chair of the board is Ane Uggla, Mærsk Mc-Kinney Møller's daughter, who took over the position in 2012 after her father passed away. The legacy of Mærsk's values is thus consciously preserved as an important asset, living on across generations.

Espoused values are indeed deeply relevant to operational decision-making. One example is Mærsk Line's decision to avoid pushing sales- and other business-related content through its new online platforms. Instead, it chose to engage its stakeholders by sharing powerful narratives that underscored the Mærsk brand's human face.[16]

Mærsk's contribution to Denmark has been substantial – from being instrumental in the post-war recovery in the 1950s, to making up a significant percentage of the country's GDP over the years. Driven by the recognition of a shortage of industry-specific skill sets, which threatens long-term industry competitiveness, Mærsk Mc-Kinney Møller has made generous donations to secondary schools. The company has also supported public projects in Denmark, for example donating $500 million for the Copenhagen opera house. But it has not limited its scope to just Denmark. Its donation targets include premier institutions of higher learning across Europe, including a CHF 15 million donation to IMD. Additionally, it is investing in building capabilities in emerging markets, in order to address gaps. In Angola, it joined forces with other partners to set up the Maritime Training Centre. These are just a few examples of how Mærsk has sought to be a driver of social good around the world.

The importance that Mærsk Mc-Kinney Møller placed on long-term reputation and conservatism is well summed up in one of the lessons he shared with the younger generations of his family: "Don't be smart in the negative sense of the word. Don't go for the quick win if it isn't a sound option for the long run. Otherwise it may impact our name."[17] These conservative principles have served Mærsk well over 50 years.

Haier: Creative Destruction

In the early 1980s, many companies in China faced a daunting challenge. Their background was one of collective ownership, but what they shared with the Tata experience described earlier was the existential "point of no return" – the frightening realization that without radical change, their management systems and product portfolios were doomed to fail. Strategies that had once been considered viable and acceptable in the old, closed market of non-existent competition and illusory consumer choice would inevitably crumble once confronted with the outside world.

In 1984, after the municipal government in the city of Qingdao in eastern China's Shandong province appointed Zhang Ruimin as general manager of the Qingdao Refrigerator Plant, he travelled to Germany to visit the company's technology partner. The experience was eye opening. Zhang Ruimin and his team realized there was a huge gap to be closed in skills, quality, and management if the company was going to survive, let alone compete internationally. As a local manufacturer operating in a country still awakening from the tumults of previous decades, their company had low-quality standards, a poor reputation and heavy debts. In fact, many of its products had to be repaired before they could be used for the first time. What China-made products shared at this time was low cost, limited technology input and a reputation for inconsistent quality.

Desperate times called for desperate measures. Facing an environment characterized by such adversity, Zhang's decisive actions to spur Haier toward his vision of the future company were courageous. In a now famous move, Zhang ordered staff at his factory to take a sledgehammer to the dozens of refrigerators (nearly 20 percent of stock) that had been found faulty or unserviceable. This was no trivial matter, considering that at a cost of several years' wages, a new refrigerator was a status symbol for many Chinese households, especially those in the countryside. With this collective catharsis behind them, Zhang and his team never looked back. They pushed through reforms that were unprecedented by the standards of Chinese collectively owned enterprises. They succeeded in their bold effort to link compensation to individual performance and to put forward incentives for improved quality control.

In his openness to understanding and acknowledging the quality gap between their products and those manufactured in the West, Zhang demonstrated a willingness to learn from others. His dramatic action left no doubt in anyone's mind about his commitment to transforming Haier. As a result, the company's sales between 1984 and 2000 grew from RMB 3.48 million to RMB 40.60 billion.

In 1993, Zhang was named CEO of the company, now renamed the Haier Group. To propel international expansion, he reorganized the workforce, from linear, functional structures into hundreds of largely autonomous internal units free to select their own leaders and compete with other units for talent and specialized projects.[18]

Convinced that Haier would do better with project teams formed according to market demands, made up of members from multiple divisions, Zhang reoriented the teams toward customer needs and the market rather than satisfying an internal bureaucracy.[19] Frontline workers were empowered to collect ideas from customers and report these to management.

The company also set up a number of manufacturing plants overseas including in the United States. Through his willingness to mobilize employees around a compelling vision, Zhang was able to inspire and influence the company to surpass other white goods manufacturers. He described his view in the following way: "Employees today should be encouraged to think for themselves. They should be cultivated to have an entrepreneurial, innovative spirit, and not just to implement orders."[20]

Pushing through such momentous and comprehensive change would have been impossible for a single executive. From the early days at a loss-making, low-quality refrigerator manufacturer, Zhang nurtured a strong management team. This allowed him to use the most unlikely of environments – a collectively owned enterprise in a provincial setting – to conceptualize and implement an entire range of radical management innovations.

In 2014, Haier's revenues were $32.8 billion. Once a very nearly bankrupt, unknown refrigerator company, it has been transformed into a global household name and the world's fourth largest, and fastest growing, white appliances manufacturer. Where other companies failed, Zhang Ruimin's team succeeded due to a compelling vision that stretched far beyond Haier's original factory. It drew on a desire to learn, improve, and make things better not only for Haier's customers but also ultimately for all of China's consumers. The process by which it achieved this is credited by many as being tremendously innovative. His commitment to drive such transformational change in a context fraught with constraints is an excellent example of leading with impact.

The Toyota Way: Lean but People-Centric

A different variety of expertise in supply chain management – one whose focus was on the speed and flexibility of in-house manufacturing processes – had been the power behind the rise of one of the world's top automakers, Toyota. Like Haier, Toyota's success came from adopting Western methods of mass production but skillfully adjusting them to an Asian context.

Although it may be difficult to believe it today, in the early post-war decades, the "made in Japan" model was widely associated with a low-cost and low-quality approach to manufacturing. Eiji Toyoda, nephew of Toyota's founder Sakichi Toyoda and cousin of Kiichiro Toyoda who established Toyota's first automobile plant in the 1930s, visited Ford auto factories in the United States in the 1950s. He realized that to make Toyota's production system viable, it would need to be reinvented from scratch.

Eiji Toyoda founded the company's technology division. He worked closely with Kiichiro Toyoda, whose vision it had been to produce a people's car; the company president Taizo Ishida; and, later, with the company's eighth president and future chairman, Hiroshi Okuda.

It was Kiichiro Toyoda's idea, in the 1930s, to expand the car engine business, which had been just an offshoot of the family's established textile loom company, into a standalone unit. Collectively, this team instilled in the Toyota workforce the culture of looking from the outside in, adopting a competitor's perspective and actively searching for weak spots that could be strengthened through better processes.

Eiji Toyoda spearheaded the formulation of the Toyota Way which became instrumental in shaping the style and philosophy of mass production and assembly line manufacturing around the world. He also pioneered the concept of kaizen – incremental but steady improvements in manufacturing and quality. As a result of these initiatives, the company's annual car sales grew from 7000 in the 1950s to almost 3.5 million by the mid-1980s.

The Toyota Way is frequently cited as lean management best practice. However, it is much more than this. Consider its first principle: "Base your management decisions on a long-term philosophy, even at the expense of short-term financial goals."[21] While many in the West today think of Eiji Toyoda almost exclusively in terms of the "lean" precepts of management and product assembly, his ideas were centered on humans and based on good stewardship. His vision was to achieve superior business performance through people. Rather than assign factory staff – managers, engineers, assembly-line workers – their places as replaceable cogs in the machine, the Toyota system was rooted in and designed along the workers' individual as well as group powers of observation, critical judgment, and natural inclination to improve and enhance the end result of their effort.

In Eiji Toyoda's own words: "People are the most important asset of Toyota, and the determinant of the rise and fall of Toyota."[22] And, in a message to Toyota managers, he said: "I want you to use your own heads. And I want you actively to train your people on how to think for themselves."[23]

Its empowered workforce, long-term focus, and lean management discipline allowed Toyota to withstand the early-1970s oil shocks better than most other automobile manufacturers for many reasons – including that it was not burdened by the costs and inventories associated with batch-and-queue processing. Its people practices considered employees as knowledge workers, whom they stimulated with cognitive problem-solving challenges. This demonstrated a clear commitment to meaningful development of human talent.[24]

The Toyota Way laid the foundation for the company's culture of stewardship as exercised by Eiji Toyoda and his team, particularly through its emphasis on long-term vision; respect for people; and addressing the roots of problems rather than their surface manifestations. Its discipline together with its long-term, all-encompassing perspective did not stop with positioning Toyota as a powerhouse in the global auto industry. Through its focus and commitment to achieving the purpose that it clearly set itself, Toyota blazed a trail in pulling Japanese brands and, by extension, Japan's national economy, out of the stagnant, no-name, low-cost, low-quality space they had occupied as a consequence of wartime destruction. It was instrumental in overcoming the country's sense of defeat as well as softening its strongly insular outlook on the world. As such, Toyoda's impact was far-reaching in terms of Japanese society, as well as the company's impressive financial achievements, which withstood the bumps and shocks of time.

Berkshire Hathaway: Far-sighted Investing

One of the world's most famous investors is Warren Buffett, CEO of Berkshire Hathaway. Over and over again, when asked for investment advice, he has cautioned individual investors against expecting quick rewards. His long-term orientation is neatly summarized in the advice he dispenses to investors: "Ignore the chatter, keep your costs minimal, and invest in stocks as you would a farm."

The way Buffett treats two of his smaller investments is illustrative of his distinctive approach. In 1986, he bought a farm in Nebraska (despite knowing nothing about farming) and in 1993 he acquired commercial real estate near New York University. Over the years, Buffett's sole consideration was productivity of these assets rather than the prospective price change. Both of these investments have paid off handsomely. In his annual letter in 2014, Buffett described the two investments as solid and satisfactory holdings for his lifetime and, subsequently, for his children and grandchildren.

Warren Buffett's selection of assets is firmly grounded in a holistic, long-term view. It is the businesses and their activities that catch his eye, rather than the quarterly earnings. Buffett explained his approach to investing in the stock market: "I look at [it] as a way to buy businesses; not to buy little things that jig, go up and down and that have charts attached to them and all that sort of thing."[25] On several occasions, Buffett has acknowledged that his business has an affinity for family-owned companies, as they share a "long-term orientation, belief in hard work and a no-nonsense approach and respect for a strong corporate culture."[26]

Buffett formed his management philosophy through hands-on experience, including working with textiles (Berkshire Hathaway), banking (Salomon Brothers), and insurance (GEICO, General Re) companies. He also oversees a number of businesses in which Berkshire Hathaway is the majority shareholder – sweet shops, furniture, executive jets, soft drinks, and others. Buffett is adamant about the value gained from getting involved in the reality of running a business, as he expressed in the following way: "Can you really explain to a fish what it's like to walk on land? One day on land is worth a thousand years of talking about it, and one day running a business has exactly the same kind of value."

Berkshire Hathaway compensates executives based on their performance in their direct areas of responsibility: higher sales, reduced expenses, or curtailed capital expenditures. Compensation is paid in cash – neither stock nor options have ever been used as management compensation. This is aligned with Buffett's strong belief in the freedom of the individual to allocate his or her resources.

When acquiring a business, Warren Buffett takes a hard look at the quality of management. Essentially, he is looking for stewards. Management should be rational and candid, and should have courage to resist the so-called "institutional imperative," i.e., the tendency of managers to engage in herd mentality. He describes how a brief letter convinced him to enter into a new (in this case overseas) partnership: "I usually know within five minutes if I'm going to make a deal. The letter gave the basic facts and told me something about the person who ran it – I could see in my mind a man with a passion for his business."[27]

In assessing managers, Buffett looks for managers who behave and think like an owner of the company. Central to this is the courage to discuss failure and mistakes openly. In his letters to investors and on his company website, Buffett openly confesses to mistakes he has made in the past, matter-of-factly describing some of them as "stupid." This is in line with his view that investing is a fundamentally human undertaking. As such, it is never quite free from psychological and emotional impulses as well as attachments – overconfidence, optimism, belief, perseverance – which may be counter-productive in achieving an investor's objectives.

Central to Berkshire's management principle is autonomy. Managers are free to run the business as they see fit. Many Berkshire subsidiaries – including Brooks, GEICO, Dairy Queen, Johns Manville, Lubrizol, and Shaw – issue formal sustainability reports on their treatment of stakeholders.[28] In 2014, Warren Buffett announced that Berkshire Hathaway would double the $15 billion that it had invested in green energy. The company has been making large investments in wind and solar power for several years.[29] While this is clearly a business decision, it is also consistent with driving social good.

But it is through his donations to charitable causes that Buffett clearly aims to achieve a lasting and positive impact on society. Going well beyond the Giving Pledge, Buffett has committed to donating 99 percent of his wealth to charity, through the Bill and Melinda Gates Foundation and other foundations. Buffett will leave a lasting mark – not in money, but in values, people, and philosophy. Among those is individual choice – we are free to change the world the way we want.

Hyundai and the Korean Miracle

The story of Hyundai Group's founder Chung Ju-yung (1915–2001) is a compelling tale of persistence and overcoming entrenched hardship to build Korea's largest business empire, an achievement that played a central role in Korea's industrialization and economic development. Chung has become a symbol of modern Korea, epitomizing the country's entrepreneurship and can-do spirit. Chung's success ultimately came from combining his strong leadership and knowledge of the Korean workforce with the logic and dictates of the government's economic planning. His achievements were all the more remarkable considering that in the late 1950s and 1960s, South Korea was recovering from damage suffered during WWII as well as the trauma of the Korean War (1950–1953). The impoverished society's economy was in ruins; life expectancy was less than 50 years. Against these monumental odds, and equipped only with primary-level education, Chung correctly anticipated the huge effort that would be required to extricate Korea from its privation. From the outset, he believed that businesses should serve a larger goal than making a profit. He viewed his new enterprise as a tool to build the nation, although this did not spare him many future confrontations with the Korean government.

In 1947, Chung Ju-yung set up Hyundai Engineering & Construction ("hyundai" meaning "modern"), the lynchpin entity within the future Hyundai conglomerate. The company grew to become the largest family-run chaebol (conglomerate) in South Korea. Its 50 subsidiaries included Hyundai Heavy Industries, Hyundai Motor, and Hyundai Electronics. Another subsidiary, Hyundai Civil Industries, won several major government contracts and was responsible for building much of Korea's transport infrastructure in the 1960s and 1970s. In the 1980s, Chung was instrumental in reorienting the national economy from large government projects to consumer-focused segments. At the height of its diversity in the late 1990s, the Hyundai Group posted annual sales of more than $80 billion. The company was an engine of Korea's rapid economic development.

During the post-war reconstruction, Chung made good use of his brother In-yung's personal network. In-yung could speak English and was on friendly terms with a number of American military officers. Later, when growing Hyundai into a dominant conglomerate, Chung drew on the ideas of a close circle of associates, including his brother Chung Se-yung, founder of Hyundai Motors, and his sons: Chung Mong-koo, head of the Hyundai Kia Automotive Group, currently honorary vice-president of FIFA; Chung Mong-hun, at one point chairman of Hyundai Group; and Chung Mong-joon, the controlling shareholder of Hyundai Heavy Industries.

Chung Ju-yung had a powerful vision for building a shipbuilding industry in Korea. He persisted with his idea in the face of public ridicule since Korea lacked the capital, technology, and experience.

He pitched the idea to foreign banks and was refused. But he managed to inspire the chairman of Barclays Bank in the United Kingdom with his description of *geobukseon* ("turtle ship"), an iron-clad battleship the Koreans had built and used to great military effect in the 16th century. He was thus able to secure the investment needed to launch the shipbuilding industry. He also persuaded a major shipping agent in Greece to place an initial order for two 2.6 million ton vessels.

In launching the highly successful shipping industry, Hyundai played a critical role in establishing Korea's industrial base. Chung's vision, ability to inspire others, persistence, and drive enabled him to positively influence the course of Korean economic progress, radically improving the capability of many members of Korean society to improve their own lives and transition into greater prosperity.

Political Stewardship: Broadening the Contextual Frame

While the focus of our discussion has been on steward leaders in business, compelling examples of stewardship can also be found in the broader context of national leadership, where it has transformed entire economies and touched the lives of millions.

For example, leading China from its disruptive 1970s upheavals and destructive social experiments to become a leading force in international trade and business required extraordinary skills, judgment, and foresight. The sheer magnitude and complexity of the task, and the very real risk of getting it wrong, probably have few precedents in modern history. Much of the credit of such a feat in China's modern history can be attributed to the team led by its "paramount leader" from 1979 to 1992, Deng Xiaoping.[30] Indeed, many historians have asked whether any other leader in the 20th century did more to improve the lives of so many or whether any other leader had such a large and lasting influence.[31]

Introducing "socialism with Chinese characteristics," Deng oversaw the transition of a nearly disintegrated society to stability, growth, and prosperity – in stark contrast to Mikhail Gorbachev's roughly concurrent and seemingly failed program to revitalize the Soviet Union.

During the Cultural Revolution, Deng had been removed from all positions of power. Yet, beginning in 1979, he led the country through a period of remarkable transformation. He instituted a program of economic reforms; paid an official visit to the United States; and saw the United States establish diplomatic relations with China (previously, Taiwan was considered the legitimate political and diplomatic representative of China).

Deng summarized and popularized his leadership as *gaige kaifang* (reform and opening up) and four modernizations (of agriculture, industry, science and technology, and military). "There are no fundamental contradictions between a socialist system and a market economy," he boldly asserted.[32] This was accompanied by his famous aphorism: "It doesn't matter whether the cat is black or white, as long as it catches mice."[33]

For impartial, well-thought-out opinion on Deng's leadership style and personal legacy, scholars of political science often quote the founding father of modern Singapore and one of Asia's most-respected statesmen, Lee Kuan Yew. "I would say the greatest [man I have met] was Deng Xiaoping. At his age, to admit that he was wrong, that all these ideas, Marxism, Leninism, Maoism, they are just not working and have to be abandoned, you need a great man to do that," said Lee Kuan Yew.[34]

Like Deng Xiaoping, Lee Kuan Yew was a great steward leader. While Deng Xiaoping influenced a large country with a population exceeding a billion, Lee Kuan Yew's stewardship impact is reflected in his leadership of a small country. But his achievement in transforming the newly independent Singapore from a third-world to a first-world nation in his lifetime is no less remarkable.

In March 2015, Lee Kuan Yew passed away at the age of 91. Concluding his funeral service eulogy, his son, Prime Minister Lee Hsien Loong, cited the quotation on the monument for Sir Christopher Wren, the architect of St Paul's Cathedral in London: "*Monumentum requiris, circumspice* – if you seek his monument, look around you." He added: "Mr. Lee Kuan Yew built Singapore."

Lee Kuan Yew could not have built modern Singapore alone. But his stewardship inspired a team of able, dedicated leaders, and galvanized a population facing a bleak outlook to survive and excel. His great achievement was to turn a small, resource-poor country into a regional leader in per capita income as well as a global hub of high-value-added financial and business services.

Several crisis points in Singapore's 20th-century history had shaped Lee Kuan Yew's social and political outlook. The 1942 fall of Singapore, a prized British colonial outpost, to Japanese occupation made Lee and other educated residents of Singapore realize that a post-war return to colonial rule was unlikely. Then in 1965, the experiment in joining freshly decolonized Singapore and Malaya into a single nation Malaysia came to an abrupt end. This reduced Singapore overnight to its circumstances of severely limited land size, labor pool and basic resources, including water.

The team of leaders representing Lee Kuan Yew's People's Action Party (PAP) overcame the 1965 crisis and its outcomes by reflecting deeply on the essence and logic of Singapore's history, particularly the strengths that had stood its immigrant communities in good stead. They committed themselves to instilling in the local population a spirit of confidence, industriousness, and self-reliance. In addition, Lee and his close associates from across the country's racial spectrum believed that a country's size, though not inconsequential, was not the be-all and end-all, and could be overcome by demonstrating greatness in its other attributes. Furthermore, they realized that a good understanding of global trends and needs would in many situations turn Singapore's vulnerability as a small and remote territory into a competitive strength.

"No one owes us a living, there is no such thing as a free lunch," Lee Kuan Yew reflected.[35] He and his colleagues understood and believed that with a combination of forward planning, resolute action, and consistent learning, Singapore could one day catapult itself into a position of excellence.

Domestically and on the world stage, Lee Kuan Yew was not afraid of making unpopular but necessary decisions, even at the risk of being branded as authoritarian. He challenged and resisted social and political trends that were popular at the time (socialism, big government, dominant labor unions), knowing that in the long term, these did not offer a way forward for his country.

He understood that neither politics nor economics played out in a social vacuum, and that racial, religious, and language tensions, if left unchecked, could bring down the entire Singapore edifice. He often acted to pre-empt and minimize conflict among the island nation's different communities, and promoted harmony where there was common space.

Faith in his countrymen's capability and resilience allowed him to execute a number of far-reaching policy changes that posed high risks yet were inevitable in his mind to secure Singapore's long-term prosperity and sustained competitiveness. In Lee Kuan Yew's words: "We were fortunate we had this cultural backdrop, the belief in thrift, hard work, filial piety and loyalty in the extended family, and, most of all, the respect for scholarship and learning."[36]

His far-sighted initiatives included: introducing a nationwide public housing program; encouraging higher birth rates in a reversal of prior policy; offering permanent resident status to skilled migrants; inviting foreign direct investment (FDI) as far back as the early 1970s; and later engineering a shift away from manufacturing. As a result, Singapore today is synonymous worldwide with excellence, reliability, safety, and best practices.

If stewardship is about handing over what one inherited in better shape to the next generation, then Lee Kuan Yew was indeed a steward leader par excellence.

While we look at examples of individual stewardship in this book in order to better understand and illustrate the key ingredients and dynamics at play, stewardship can also occur at the organizational level. Values can be embedded into processes and frameworks in order to build a context that is conducive to stewardship. As such, many of the key stewardship concepts that we discuss can also apply in an organizational context. The quality of governance impacts the degree to which stewardship is fostered – or not.

Switzerland is an example of organizational stewardship at the national level. With a stable, prosperous, and high-tech economy, Switzerland is frequently ranked as the wealthiest country in the world, in per capita terms. It has the world's 19th largest economy by nominal GDP and is the 20th largest exporter, despite its small size. In 2014, it was ranked the second most competitive economy by the IMD World Competitiveness Yearbook.[37] Despite the recent economic crisis, its economy has grown at a steady pace and its unemployment rate in 2015 was 3.2 percent. This is all the more impressive considering its dearth of natural resources, its relatively small population (8 million), and the added complexity of cultural diversity (as demonstrated by its four national languages).

Its success in the face of the downturn has been attributed to rising productivity, a balanced government budget and small debt burden, as well as low borrowing costs. Switzerland also has the highest household savings rate in the developed world and relatively little economic inequality. Its business-friendly tax system is attractive to foreign investment. With a political system built on direct democracy, populist proposals can be voted down in nationwide referendums.

Through its prudence in considering the long term when making policies that affect business, involvement of the populace in direct democracy, and fostering an environment in which power and benefits are distributed, Switzerland creates an inclusive context for engaged and productive citizens. As such, Switzerland provides an inspiring example of what can be achieved when sound organizational stewardship is in place.

CHAPTER 2

Stewardship Principles

Chapter 1 highlights some outstanding steward leaders. However, as we have seen, stewardship is not entirely dependent on great efforts by individual leaders. We briefly discussed organizational stewardship at the end of Chapter 1. Now we examine in clearer focus what is core to well-stewarded organizations in building the resilience needed to navigate the bumps and shocks of reality – especially in the rapidly evolving context of emerging markets. We shall explore the evolution of stewardship. In the process, we identify the key principles that underpin the concept and its practice, to help us make sense of the stories and examples highlighted.

Stewardship has its theoretical roots in several different traditions. Within normative ethics (the branch of ethics that examines what constitutes moral actions), deontological thinkers believe that a morally correct action needs to consider, at the same time, one's duties and the rights of others, and that this is universally applicable.[1] The German philosopher Immanuel Kant offers a philosophical categorization of our basic ethical obligations to others, the so-called "categorical imperative." According to this, people are not a means to an end, but an end in and of themselves. Considering the impact of our actions across society then becomes necessary.

The notion of treating people with respect resonates with the many systems of ethics around the world. The inter-connectivity of all human life, and the human duty to act in a way that is respectful of the environment and other members of the community, including future generations, is common to many philosophies and traditions. The Bible, the Torah, the Qur'an, the Hindu Vedas, and the Buddhist scriptures all make reference to the notion of stewardship, with the connotation of managing or looking after entrusted property. Buddhist scholars in Thailand have pointed out that Buddhist concepts such as "loving kindness" are based on a thought of "giving," whereas the standard international discourse of laws and seeking protection of one's rights reflect a metaphor of "taking."[2]

In everyday usage, a steward is commonly used to refer to a person who looks after passengers on a train, ship, or airplane. This associates the notion of service with stewardship.

In a corporate context the term stewardship has been used to embrace a variety of meanings and connotations. These have drawn on several elements identified in philosophy and religion, including accountability, a long-term orientation, and responsibility for protecting assets over time. In the business sense, the focus is less on the service dimension that often characterizes the spiritual concept of stewardship. Instead, the focus is more on a sense of oneself being responsible to a context greater than simply the individual or company level, and to a longer time horizon, which sometimes even extends beyond one lifetime.

Shaping Stewardship

Stewardship has a critical and irreplaceable role to play in effecting change. Stewardship can re-energize the way in which we look at how we can affect our sphere of influence, at the individual, organizational, and societal level.

An aid in understanding stewardship in a corporate context is, perhaps ironically, agency theory. This separates a firm's ownership from its management. The principal (usually the owner or main shareholder) designates an agent who is expected to act in the former's best interest.[3] When there is a misalignment between the interests of the principal and the agent, and when the principal lacks sufficient information to be able to understand the agent's performance, the result is an agency problem.[4] Agency theory assumes that individuals are primarily motivated to behave in ways that maximize benefits for themselves. In practice this means organizational rewards and punishments are needed to incentivize managers so that they behave in ways that support the owner's goals.

Stewardship theory is a contrasting concept of motivation that grew out of organizational psychology and organizational sociology. According to this theory, people are motivated by a need to achieve and to gain intrinsic satisfaction through successfully performing challenging work and exercising responsibility and authority. Even in cases where a course of action is unrewarding personally, managers will be motivated to go ahead and undertake the task out of a sense of duty.[5] According to former President and CEO of Mitsubishi Corporation, Minoru Makihara: "The free market is the best system for allocating resources, but never forget that it has to be supported by integrity, compassion, and a sense of social responsibility."[6]

Stewardship theory predicts that managers will act in ways that protect the assets they control on behalf of the owners. Since stewards identify themselves with the business and are motivated to maximize organizational performance, they behave in ways that benefit the business and its owners. The way to ensure that they continue to be motivated to do their best is by giving them free rein to act.

The different factors that prompt motivation vary. At the individual level, why are some individuals more motivated to act as stewards than others? One explanation is that people who are motivated by higher order needs (or "self-actualization needs" in Abraham Maslow's motivational framework) are more likely to act as organizational stewards.[7] This means that there is a greater probability that intrinsically motivated individuals – those who are driven by an interest or enjoyment in doing the work itself and are motivated from within rather than by external pressures or a desire for reward – will be stewards. This is a common theme in the emerging economies where many business and industry leaders perform their roles not because of monetary rewards, but because they seek a sense of personal and organizational achievement, the challenge of making things happen in an under-developed institutional framework, and the opportunity to apply a lifetime's worth of practical experience and insight.

How strongly an individual identifies with the organization is another prompt for stewardship behavior. This means that the more an individual perceives that the company's core identity intersects with their view of themselves, the more they are likely to personalize organizational success or failure. This cascades down the organization. There is evidence that organizational identification is directly related to employee performance.[8] Of course, in the extreme scenario, a business leader, particularly in a family-owned business, not only identifies with the company – for all intents and purposes, he or she often is the company.

A related factor is value commitment. This is defined as belief in and acceptance of the goals of the organization (or its corporate purpose). Higher value commitment predicts that executives will be more likely to act as organizational stewards.[9]

When executives use personal power as a basis for influencing others, rather than relying on institutional power, they are more likely to be stewards.[10] This suggests that people who cultivate personal relationships and influence will be more likely to be stewards than those who pull rank and rely on their formal authority. In some societies, such as the majority of Asian countries, the act of business leaders wielding personal power is made easier by a relative lack of barriers between professional and personal domains, and by the strong emphasis on personal interactions rather than institutional procedures.

Context also clearly plays a role. Cultural and societal factors, as well as organizational frameworks, are relevant in considering social norms and forces that may be encouraging or hindering stewardship from emerging in a given context. While we caution against generalizations, there is some evidence that institutional collectivism (i.e., a sense of connection to society as a whole, rather than an in-group such as a family) encourages the emergence of stewardship.

Another relevant cultural dimension is power distance, the degree to which people with less power in a society accept the unequal distribution of power. In cultures where power distance is great, hierarchy is often the norm in organizations, and those higher up in the hierarchy tend to make decisions with little consultation of subordinates. We will discuss these concepts in greater detail.

The reality is that a number of social, organizational, and individual factors affect how likely it is for stewardship to emerge in a given organization (see Table 2.1). Agency and stewardship orientation may even co-exist, with some parts of the organization operating more along agency principles, while others function predominantly on stewardship principles.[11] For example, a call center for a software company may be driven by contractual obligations and have financial incentives for employees linked to performance indicators. However, in motivating its talent – for example, its star application developers who are often courted by many other companies – the same company may motivate them more as stewards, helping them build identification with organizational goals to increase their sense of ownership and contribution to the overall goals.

Table 2.1   Characteristics of agency versus stewardship orientation at the individual, organizational, and social level

Dimension	Agency orientation	Stewardship orientation
Scope of group identification	Restricted to immediate social groups (in-group)	Extended to societal collective as a whole
Degree of power distance	High power distance	Low power distance
Organizational		
Source of power (emphasis)	Institutional power (legitimate, coercive, reward)	Personal power (expert, referent)
Basis for relationship	Contractual	Trust
Corporate purpose	Defined in financial terms	Beyond profit
Leadership	Transactional, performance-based, low level of trust in subordinates, short-term view	Transformational/emotional engagement with employees, a high level of trust in subordinates, long-term view
Rationale for leadership action	Incentives	Values
On whose behalf is the leader acting?	Shareholder	Beyond shareholders
Governance structure	CEO versus Board (check and balance)	CEO and Board (alignment)
Individual		
Psychological (motivation)	Extrinsic, lower order needs	Intrinsic, higher order needs
Identification with the organization	Low	High
Commitment to organizational goals	Low value	High value

Source: IMD Research (2014), multiple sources.

The Reality of Stewardship

The evolution of stewardship has many strands. But, as the examples in the opening chapter illustrate, what is important is how stewardship delivers value to individuals, organizations, and society today and in the future. Reinforced by our quantitative study, we identified three key dimensions of stewardship:

- Leading with impact
- Safeguarding the future
- Driving social good.

Leading with impact

To better understand and test our hypothesis of stewardship, we conducted an empirical study aimed at exploring the narrative of stewardship, its correlation with certain key performance indicators, and the implications.

The results of our research were striking. When we consider financial leverage, for example, companies ranking in the bottom quartile have 50 percent more debt than companies ranking in the upper-most quartile. In examining the results of our word content analysis, the difference in word usage related to leadership values and behaviors is also clear. Companies potentially ranking higher on stewardship used words like *ambition, challenge, contribution, independent, integrity, responsibility, steward, trustee, vision,* and *wealth.* As such, the narrative of well-stewarded companies seems to place greater emphasis on achieving impact (*aim, ambition, challenge, effort*), societal responsibility (*duties, integrity, responsibility, relevance, roles*), and long-termism (*safeguard, steward, sustainably, trustee, vision*).

Stewardship is a process that is distinctive in terms of what drives it, how it is enacted by the various actors involved, and the impact it has on a range of spheres and over time. Figure 2.1 summarizes the inter-relationship between the various dimensions of stewardship.

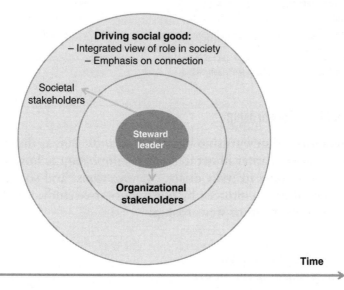

Figure 2.1   Stewardship spheres

Steward leaders are a key driver of stewardship. But what makes a steward leader? Examining the values and beliefs of recognized leaders, we better understand what motivates their approach to leadership – and whether this is influenced by cultural programming. We explore the underlying psychological traits of the steward leaders: Is there something characteristic about their personalities? Is there something specific in their make-up that explains their willingness to build businesses with such ambition and drive and that enables them to spread their view to others? Is there something particular in the evolution of their experiences that lends them the tenacity to build organizations with such a long-term view? What underlies their commitment to ensuring that the organizations they build are not at the cost of the societies around them, but rather enrich all who are part of their ecosystem?

Many stewards refer to critical transitions while they were growing up as providing their inspiration. Whether it is their internal value set or personality that motivates them, it is their actions and the effects of their actions that matter. Through their ability to create meaning through stories, build trust, and foster organizational knowledge-sharing, steward leaders create a strong internal cohesiveness. They prime their organizations to act in ways that benefit the external world. By articulating what value the organization adds through its core activities, as well as how it is able to reinforce the fabric of the communities in which it operates, stewards build a clear understanding of the company's commitment to contributing over the longer term.

How does a leader become a steward leader? By looking at the capabilities stewards cultivate at a granular level, we explore the practices that characterize their leadership style to ensure their organizations deliver real impact – in the financial and social sense. We also examine how they ensure that they are building the organizational capacity and resilience needed to continue to deliver impact over time. This includes ensuring succession and inspiring other stewards. Stewardship is not without its dangers. There are clear risks that stewards need to actively manage to ensure that the organization's future is safeguarded.

Steward leaders are driven by a clear conviction of what purpose the firm should serve and their own values and integrity in the way they treat their people. They are highly effective at mobilizing and engaging the people inside the organization and at building employee ownership and commitment to contributing their utmost. They pay close attention to the people who work for them, endeavoring to ensure a close alignment between the organizational processes and its purpose and values. Again our word content analysis is revealing: companies that potentially rank high on stewardship used words like *career, colleagues, commitment, compensation, engaging, grooming, promoting, recognizing,* and *talent.* They seem to have a long-term view of their people, nurturing their development, with a focus on recognition and engagement.

One example of a leader who placed people firmly at the center of his management philosophy is Panasonic Group's founder Konosuke Matsushita (1894–1989). Matsushita dreamed of using technological progress as a means of escaping poverty ever since the introduction of electricity. Growing the company into one of the world's largest manufacturers of electrical goods, along the way popularizing brand names such as National, Panasonic, Technics, and Quasar, and reaching an annual turnover of $65 billion were accomplishments requiring great resilience, boundless discipline, a willingness to take risks, and self-sacrifice.

As the company grew in size, Matsushita realized that all employees should adhere to a set of written guiding principles. The company introduced "Matsushita's seven spirits" (at the time largely unheard of in the business community):

1. Service to the public
2. Fairness and honesty
3. Teamwork
4. Unity of corporate and personal effort
5. Courtesy and humility
6. Accordance with natural laws
7. Gratitude for blessings.

Matsushita firmly believed that a business as large as his had a responsibility to help all of society prosper. He cared deeply for the employees of his company as if they were family, and provided the majority of them with the option of lifetime employment within the group of companies. His words demonstrate his care for his employees: "I shall not dismiss a single employee, I shall reduce working time to half a day and cut production by half but I'll continue to pay a full day's wages. In return, store employees will give up their holidays and do everything in their power to sell the goods we have in stock."[12]

Matsushita's soft-spoken and self-deprecating character may partly explain why little was known in the West of his management theories until books on the Matsushita brand of leadership started to appear in the late 1990s. Since then many management thinkers have spoken of Konosuke Matsushita as an authentic leader who, by virtue of being true to himself, led others to be true to themselves, which typically not only improved their individual sense of well-being but also produced sizable social benefits.[13] The impact of Matsushita as a steward leader – through his relentless drive for business results, deep care for his employees, and commitment to securing Panasonic's continued success – is undeniable.

In addition to deeply caring about employees and understanding other organizational stakeholders, steward leaders seek to understand the needs of the external stakeholders who are important to the mid- and long-term success of the company. By contributing positively to the societal context, steward leaders drive social good and carve out a positive role for the organization.

Nestlé calls its way of doing business "Creating Shared Value," which holds that in order to be successful over the long term and create value for shareholders, it must create value for society. According to Nestlé CEO Paul Bulcke, at the core of the global debt crisis was a values crisis. Bulcke commented that "too many people and businesses had been seduced by or pressured into delivering on short-term egoistic targets and there was a general shift in thinking towards 'me-now' instead of 'us-tomorrow.'" Leaders need to show, through their actions, the importance which they attribute to the fundamental role of business, which is, in Bulcke's words: "value creation for society as a whole with a long-term perspective."[14]

Safeguarding the future

A well-stewarded organization is focused on not only delivering current performance without compromising future impacts in terms of earnings but also ensuring the continuity of the capabilities and relationships that form the basis of its ability to create future value. Success can, therefore, be measured as the net positive impact on future generations in terms of economic, social, and environmental performance. These organizations are willing to sacrifice short-term profits to secure longer-term benefits for the organization.

When Ayala Corporation, the leading industrial conglomerate – and one of the oldest – in the Philippines, received the 19th annual IMD-Lombard Odier Global Family Business Award at the 25th Summit of the Family Business Network International (FBN-I) in Dubai in 2014, it was commended for its "strongly rooted values; long-term, strategic partnerships; commitment to family leadership and stewardship; consistency of values across generations; strong belief that contributing to the nation's development was in the family's long-term business interest; and well-planned succession policies." It demonstrates a clear commitment to ensuring the continuity of its own operations and ability to create wealth over time.

One way to ensure the continuity of operations is through conservative financing. Mærsk publicly states that its policies are built on its commitment to maintaining a conservative capital structure. With a long-term focus, it raises funding from diverse sources and strives to achieve a balanced maturity profile. In so doing, it aims to have enough liquidity to be sufficiently flexible to support the growth of the business.[15]

Our study findings with regard to the difference in approaches to debt are dramatic. Companies scoring high on our Implied Stewardship Index use 50 percent less long-term debt than companies scoring low on this index (Table A.3 in the Appendix has more details). Companies with less debt are more flexible to finance projects, giving them the capacity to invest in projects that are strategic for long-term growth and resilient in the face of crisis.

This long-term thinking and ability to imagine a compelling future also mean that short-term pain is a necessary and bearable cost to achieve the goal. The findings from our word content analysis reveal striking differences in the usage of words related to time. Companies potentially ranking high on stewardship use words such as *long-term, continually, continuously, years, decade, decades, era, future*. In contrast, lower-scoring companies more frequently use words like *currently, daily, immediate, months, prompt, quarterly,* and *recently* (see Table 2.2).

Leading with impact also means having a vision that is daring and ambitious. This is well illustrated by the example of Taiwanese company Acer, set up in 1976 with seed capital of $25,000 raised from Stan Shih, his spouse, and five other business partners. Eager to

Table 2.2   Usage of words related to time

Companies potentially ranking high on stewardship	Companies potentially ranking low on stewardship
century, coming, constant, continually, continue, continuous, decades, era, future, long-term, moment, old, ongoing, onward, perpetual, tomorrow, year	contemporaneous, currently, daily, dates, immediate, month, monthly, months, overnight, promptly, quarterly, quarters, recently

break out of the OEM space to innovate radically, Shih realized that Taiwan's high-tech industry was in a good position to become self-reliant not only in terms of technology but also in terms of capital, management, and target markets. It also set its sights on the global rather than local marketplace. "Why don't we have the ambition?" asked Shih. "Why are we chasing the Western companies? In 50 years, why can't it be them chasing us?"[16]

Fueled by this ambition, Acer grew from being a humble start-up to a viable, international, branded business and ultimately a recognized and globally competitive player. In 2014, Acer was one of the world's four biggest PC vendors, with annual sales of $10 billion.

In order to make this incredible trajectory possible, early on Shih understood the importance of making continuous, long-term investments in research and development, marketing, and branding. His foresight in thinking about how the company would renew itself in the future inspired him to come up with new perspectives on the product lifecycle. These included the "smiling curve" – a new concept and configuration of the product lifecycle stages. The smiling curve visually captured the idea that real value-adds occurred outside either side of manufacturing, i.e., in product conceptualization, R&D, design, and branding of the product, as well as distribution, marketing, and after-sales service.

This process of cooperation is strengthened by a solid foundation of trust. Well-stewarded organizations tend to have corporate cultures where relationships are based on trust. Their strategy balances value contribution with value appropriation over time and recognizes the wider context in which the organization operates. Their structures are well adapted to the company strategy and purpose. In some cases, this means they are decentralized in order to promote a more equitable distribution of power in the company and greater initiative from the bottom.

For example, Nestlé operates in 197 countries. Its local country units work with considerable autonomy, particularly in developing products that best cater to local market preferences. This allows for a great deal of business innovation at the local level, as well as initiatives aimed at benefiting the communities in which they operate, and developing insights into the trends that will secure long-term success. For example, Nestlé Pakistan plays a central role in modernizing the dairy sector in Pakistan. As the dominant player in the milk processing industry, it has made its aim to work with rural dairy producers to increase productivity, improve market access, and promote diversified livelihoods for smallholders.

With a long-term view, well-stewarded organizations put in place structures that are resilient enough to adapt to changing circumstances. Values are deeply embedded in organizational decision-making, and processes allow for consistency of action while enabling organizational flexibility. Their people are driven by a connection to the corporate values and purpose, rewarded fairly and engaged to contribute. They understand how to best contribute their talents and energies to create company value while developing their own potential.

In addition to efficiently and effectively managing their current context, organizations that safeguard the future require the ability to balance current opportunities with investing in growth potential for the future. To make this judgment call, to strike the right balance, stewardship requires boards that are able to think strategically, actively develop a variety of mid- and long-term scenarios, and flag risks to management. A central stewardship task of boards is to secure a successor to the current steward leader to make sure that stewardship principles do not disappear when a leader moves on.

Too often, however, boards do not pay adequate attention to succession. The media abounds with stories of venerated business leaders coming out of retirement when they realize that their departure has set in motion a decline in performance. One example of missed succession is that of Infosys founder Narayana Murthy. Murthy served as the company's CEO for over 20 years and as chairman for another nine and often referred to Infosys as his child. He stepped down from the board in 2011 but, after a couple of years of shaky company performance, he returned in 2013 as executive chairman for five years. Feeding and nurturing the succession pipeline needs to be a clear priority to ensure long-term continuity and performance.

Driving social good

Firms need to play their part in building a healthy ecosystem in which stewardship can flourish. They can do this internally, by stimulating intrinsic motivation in employees, and externally, through clear links to stakeholders and the surrounding communities to cultivate a landscape of greater transparency and trust. Organizations that are well stewarded have a clear sense of where they are going and why, a strong commitment to creating wealth in both the medium and long term, and building the governance systems that foster effective exchange and supervision among the relevant actors.

When Ratan Tata used certain profits to develop the community rather than pay out dividends, he was making an investment in rural populations. He felt that this was a duty of the company: "By providing support in areas such as health and education, livelihoods and the environment, we ... take the well-being ... within our own plants and facilities to the world immediately outside them. It gives the community a sense of belonging and sharing in our growth rather than developing a distaste for us."[17]

A key underlying question is: what is the purpose of the firm? Most executives feel that they need to demonstrate consistent earnings, quarter after quarter, to meet shareholder expectations. In the 1970s and 1980s, a commonly heard view was that the purpose of the firm was to maximize shareholder returns.[18] In this view, the owners' or shareholders' interests are of primary importance and the company has a fiduciary obligation to place their needs above all others. Whether this profit maximization should be short term or long term has been the subject of further discussion. However, the idea that the firm's primary goal is to maximize its shareholder returns was a widely held one – and still is in many quarters.

In the 1980s, stakeholder theory took the view that a firm's impact on its other stakeholders – not just shareholders – is vital. Employees, customers, suppliers, financiers, governmental bodies, communities, trade unions, and industry bodies are all concerned with the firm's operations. The firm's raison d'être is to facilitate productive exchanges between stakeholders; companies that work to serve the interests of a broad group of stakeholders will create more value over time.[19] As such, the firm's responsibility extends far beyond shareholder return maximization. A number of academics, such as Lynne Stout (author of *The Shareholder Value Myth*), and business leaders, like Warren Buffett, have backed this view, pointing out the destructive consequences of maximizing shareholder value to the exclusion of all other stakeholder benefits.

Steward leaders commit themselves to building organizations that play a key role in driving social good. This was a central motivator for Ratan Tata, for example, who views the contribution of the company as building a foundation for technology and setting standards for corporate governance and ethical business conduct. It was also the driver for Filipino conglomerate Ayala to submit a proposal to take over the water concession for the metropolitan area of Manila in 1996. Despite its lack of experience, chairman and CEO Jaime Augusto Zóbel de Ayala saw proper water management as critical for the economic development of Manila – especially for the lowest income groups in the city – and that it had a contribution to make. It also inspired the company to build the Ayala Foundation to help use its expertise to build communities.

The stewardship dimension of driving social good becomes even more pressing when we consider that up until the 2007 financial crisis, moral and ethical considerations were largely excluded from business education and theory. A vocal critic of business schools was Sumantra Ghoshal who argued that "by propagating ideologically inspired amoral theories, business schools have actively freed their students from any sense of moral responsibility."[20]

In recent years, business schools have made increasing efforts to build ethics, notions of moral responsibility, and sustainability into their curricula to help future leaders develop their sensitivity to their responsibility to contribute. It is important that business leaders understand the broader purpose of the organization and ensure that the firm's goals (of which there may be a multitude) are compatible and prioritized.[21] Composed of people who have a range of aspirations, firms are not faceless entities. Having integrity requires making sure the way that individuals make everyday decisions is consistent with their goals and aligned with their core purpose.

However, there is often a gap between the articulated purpose of a firm and managerial attitudes within it. Therefore, having an authentic corporate purpose is critical. This requires "alignment between a firm's perceived corporate purpose and the actual strategic decisions and actions it takes."[22] Having an authentic corporate purpose not only provides the focus and integrity to help drive a firm's activities consistently, it can also help firms to understand and assess whether they are having the impact they set out to deliver.

The Stewardship Landscape

Leaders drive stewardship, building relationships in a range of circles, as well as the organizational culture and capabilities to sustain it over time. But who stewards the stewards?

Other actors in the stewardship system have key roles to play in ensuring that the leader is appropriately balancing issues that are of short- and long-term strategic relevance and managing risk. Effective oversight has its part in keeping the organization on track, relying on people to perform their roles with a high degree of conscientiousness, competence, and integrity. This means that in addition to an enlightened and responsible chief executive, company owners, boards, and management have their respective roles to play in ensuring that the right governance is in place.

There is no one definitive stewardship model. We observe stewardship in many different types of ownership structures, including family, public, institutional, and state-owned. Good stewardship can be seen in private family-owned businesses such as Mars and Tata (majority owned by trusts) as well as in publicly listed companies such as Acer and Haier.

Owners

Ownership structures differ and are increasingly fragmented and complex, sometimes making the attribution of responsibilities unclear. Different ownership forms naturally lead to diverse approaches to the objectives and risks that the organization can take, and influence the ways in which stewardship is approached.

For a corporation, the business is a separate legal entity from its owners, who can be either private or government. Publicly traded for-profit corporations are owned by the shareholders. A privately owned corporation usually means the company is owned by the company's founders, management, or private investors. There are also partnerships, where two or more people own the firm; the partners have unlimited liability for the business debts. In a sole proprietorship, the business is owned by one person who has unlimited liability for all obligations. A cooperative is a limited liability business that has members as owners sharing decision-making authority.

Shareholders are the owners of a limited company; they can be individuals or companies. They provide the capital to finance firm growth. Hence they are also termed investors (increasingly institutional investors), such as pension funds. Shareholder rights depend on the class of stock held, but generally include access to information, participating in annual general meetings, and voting rights. Shareholders do not intervene in the company's operation, but they generally have one important right: to appoint and remove directors.

Owners are shareholders, investors, and principals, and often these terms are used quite interchangeably. However, a key element of stewardship is the concept of having an ownership mentality, defined by a strong sense of attachment to the business and a desire to work toward its sustained success for the longer term. Such an ownership mentality is obviously more prevalent with founder-owners and family-owned business owners as compared with investors who are merely seeking short-term returns.

Ownership also comes with responsibilities. While we frequently talk about shareholder rights, their responsibilities are rarely mentioned. Led by the development in the United Kingdom of a stewardship code in 2010, a number of other countries are developing similar codes (Japan, Singapore, South Africa, and others) to address this area and to define the scope of these responsibilities of ownership.

Boards

The board is the governing body that oversees the activities of the firm. The board sets objectives and the tone at the top of the organization. It appoints the executives, supports them, monitors performance, and ensures objectives are met. It also ensures that the firm has adequate levels of financing, approves annual budgets, and determines the compensation of the management. The board is responsible to and reports to shareholders for the organization's performance.

The legal responsibilities of the board and its members depend on the nature of the organization and the jurisdiction within which it operates. In publicly held companies board members are elected by shareholders, whereas in other settings board members can be appointed. The board usually chooses one of its members to serve as its chair. In its function as the key link between the shareholders and the firm, the board ensures that the firm has the leadership capabilities to fulfill its mandate. It typically makes decisions on behalf of the principal(s).

In fulfilling its mandate, the board engages with management to discuss strategic questions and to challenge its thinking. Two of the individuals instrumental in founding Home Depot, Ken Langone (who was a long-serving board member) and Bernard Marcus (chairman until 2002), describe how the board disagreed with management about strategic questions, for example with regard to reformulating the small-store concept, and on revisiting expansion into Latin America. The point worth noting is that neither the board nor the management "won" the argument, but rather, after an intensive exchange, they were able to find new solutions together.[23]

Management

The chief executive and the management are responsible for managing the firm's resources and operationalizing its strategy. The CEO is ultimately responsible for all day-to-day management decisions and for implementing the firm's long- and short-term plans. The CEO serves as a liaison between the board and the management of the company and communicates to the board on the management's behalf. Key to this role is the trust the CEO demonstrates in his or her board, supplying it with relevant and complete information in a timely manner. Enron's chairman and CEO never told the board that whistleblower Sherron Watkins had raised major questions about financial irregularities.

The important relationships between the owners, the board, and the management are depicted in Figure 2.2. Together, all three steward the firm, safeguarding and growing values, benefitting the firm's stakeholders and the larger community over the longer term. As trusted and responsible stewards, they seek to hand over a thriving business and organization in better shape to the next generation or to their successors.

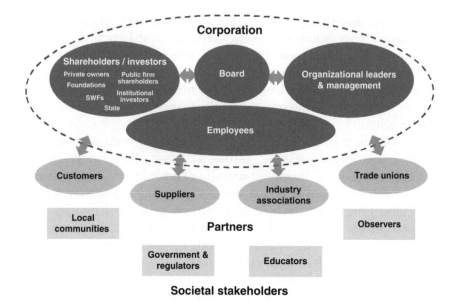

Figure 2.2   The relationship between the key actors in the stewardship ecosystem

Context: What Conditions Foster Stewardship?

In addition to the leader and other stewardship actors, the context in which the organization finds itself is also important in influencing stewardship. Culture is one key part of context. We believe that stewardship is more likely to arise in specific cultural contexts. While cultural values can be analyzed in different ways, one set of categories that we find helpful in discerning possible differences with regard to stewardship is the following:[24]

- **Environment:** Is our basic relationship with the world around us based on harmony, mastery, or subjugation?
- **Relationships:** To whom and for whom are we naturally responsible? This applies whether a culture is hierarchical, collectivist, or individually focused.
- **Activity:** What is the basic or natural approach to activity? This can be broadly categorized as being, doing, or thinking-oriented.

Geert Hofstede's work on culture is the most frequently cited in management literature with regard to how values in the workplace are influenced by culture.[25] Hofstede defines culture as "the collective programming of the mind distinguishing the members of one group or category of people from another." The two dimensions (Hofstede defines six all together) that are most relevant to stewardship are individualism vs. collectivism and power distance.

Societies with cultures that rank higher on individualism have a preference for a loosely knit social framework in which the expectation is that individuals take care of themselves and their immediate families only. On the other end of the spectrum, more collectivist cultures prefer tightly knit groups, whereby the norm is that members of a particular in-group (family or other) look after other members of the collective and expect unquestioning loyalty in return.

Power distance reflects how a society handles inequalities among people. People in societies characterized by a large degree of power distance are more accepting of a hierarchical order in which everybody has a place; in societies with low power distance, people strive to equalize the distribution of power. How does this translate? In business cultures with high power distance, subordinates are less likely to question decisions made by their boss. In lower power distance cultures, leaders may place greater value on participation from their subordinates in meetings.

At first glance, it would seem that societies that are more collectivist in culture would be more apt to promote stewardship. However, this may not necessarily be the case. It depends on the kind of collectivism. In fact, the degree to which collectivism may influence stewardship depends on which group the individual identifies with. Collectivism is multi-dimensional, which means that individuals feel affinity with different groups.[26]

Institutional collectivism refers to how much importance the culture places on the collective distribution of resources and collective action, and how much it emphasizes group performance and reward.[27] In-group collectivism means that people value their connection to their family unit or employer organization. The value here is on pride, loyalty, and cohesiveness of families or other groups.

In her recent work Martha Maznevski of IMD and her colleagues examined the relative preference of a culture for individualism vs. collectivism (see Figure 2.3) and she points out that even for countries that have relatively similar levels of collectivism vs. individualism, the group itself may change. In Figure 2.3, Australia and the United Kingdom are actually very collective, with the reference group

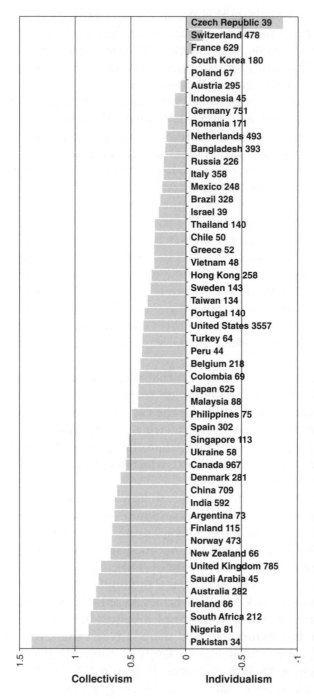

Figure 2.3   Relative preference of cultures for individualism vs. collectivism

being your "mates." China's collectivism is more around family (in-group), while Sweden's is around society as a whole (institutional). Other cultural scholars have come up with different ways of looking at this trait, for example by degree of autonomy vs. embeddedness. In highly embedded cultures, people value participating in a group and identifying with its goals, whereas cultures valuing autonomy place greater emphasis on uniqueness of the individual.

Is there a relationship between the degree of a culture's collectivism or individualism and the likelihood it will foster stewardship? One study showed that greater institutional collectivism was positively associated with all of the three following elements: (1) attention to business impact (firm profitability, sales volume); (2) stakeholder concerns (employee relations and effect on the environment); and (3) contribution to the community (welfare of the local community as well as the economic welfare of the nation).[28] Conversely, there was no such correlation with in-group collectivism or with higher levels of power distance. This seems to indicate that cultures with high levels of institutional collectivism "encourage delaying immediate needs or gratification for future concerns and priorities,"[29] and therefore reflect upon how managerial actions impact upon society more generally.

The same study found that managers in cultures valuing greater power distance tend to devalue all three of the above aspects. As such, greater power distance would seem to be less likely to promote stewardship. One explanation is that those in power may use it for their personal benefit: "Societies with higher power distance are prone to the manipulative use of power, lack of opportunities for minorities and women, lack of personal and professional developing within the organization."[30]

Greater institutional collectivism and lower power distance at the cultural level may help to foster stewardship. However, we would caution against making generalizations. Instead, it is helpful to consider the range of cultural contexts in which steward leaders operate. In emerging market contexts, where institutional gaps are often vast (lack of proper infrastructure, weak governmental institutions, poor health services, insufficient governance, inadequate schooling), steward leaders have demonstrated a willingness to address these shortcomings and to build connections with the communities in which they operate. Also, working in such a difficult context seems to have contributed to their ability to delay gratification, sacrificing short-term gain for long-term benefit. Steward leaders in companies operating in the United States and Europe have often placed greater emphasis on owners' concerns for growth and financial impact. Different contexts have led to the development of different aspects of stewardship. We are not suggesting, therefore, that one culture is more prone to fostering stewardship than another, but rather we seek to understand what it is about the steward leaders in these different contexts that has enabled them to be effective.

One thing that they have in common is their ability to adapt their leadership style to their context. This may mean conforming to cultural expectations and values of collectivism and power distance – or not – depending on what is needed (e.g., sometimes going against expectations and norms can stimulate innovation). Also, Bernard Bass's research suggests that transformational leadership may take more or less participative forms depending on power distance. In whatever way they choose to do it, steward leaders have as their ambition to build the elements of stewardship into the organization so that the organization can continue to operate successfully and responsibly over time and not be dependent on an individual leader to do so.

A number of other cultural scholars use different lenses to view and assess cultural differences. The anthropologist Edward T. Hall developed the popular concept of high and low context cultures, and the degree of resulting inferences and social inclusion and exclusion.[31] In his work, Fons Trompenaars went on to classify cultures along seven dimensions: universalism vs. particularism, individualism vs. collectivism, neutral vs. emotional, specific vs. diffuse, achievement vs. ascription, sequential vs. synchronic, and internal vs. external control.[32] Richard Lewis categorizes cultures along three poles – linear active, multi-active, and reactive – to look at the implications of cultural differences on communication, status, and hierarchy, and how this impacts teams, motivation, and leadership.[33]

The examples we have focused on in this book have been primarily in Asia. As mentioned previously, context has an important influence on the shape stewardship takes. In an emerging market context, steward leaders may fill an important institutional gap. In all countries and contexts, there are forces that promote and deter stewardship. Asian countries may be more culturally inclined to a long-term orientation. Also, with their focus on preserving harmony in social contexts, they may demonstrate greater awareness of the needs of the stakeholders around them. However, an emphasis on hierarchy and in-group loyalty may make it more difficult for change agents to take initiatives and challenge the status quo.

Social forces are in flux and management practices may be diverging from traditional values in many Asian countries. While it is important to avoid over-generalizations and simplifications, our objective in exploring this cultural dimension is to help foster cross-fertilization of the best stewardship conditions and practices across different contexts.

CHAPTER

3

Steward Leaders Inspire

By definition, stewards outlive themselves. As part of their concern with safeguarding the future, great steward leaders think beyond themselves, their organizations, and their lifetime, and are able to make short-term sacrifices for a long-term gain. In this chapter, we explore how stewardship values and attributes can be cultivated and disseminated, and how great steward leaders inspire other stewards with their actions.

Great stewards beget stewards. The visionary nature of stewardship inspires greatness in others. In *Start with Why*, Simon Sinek observes: "Great leaders lead with WHY. They embody a sense of purpose that inspires those around them."[1] However, few people or organizations articulate why they do what they do in terms of their purpose, belief, and the reason for their organization's existence. Many start with WHAT and HOW, often trying too hard to improve with a blueprint of how they are to achieve what they want to achieve. But, a compelling raison d'être – and an ability to articulate WHY clearly and succinctly – is essential. And the WHY differentiates the inspiring leaders from the merely effective ones.

Even the most cynical corporate leaders can find inspiration from the stories of great steward leaders. Buoyed by these legacies and energized by their own possibilities for contribution, stewardship stories are a powerful source of motivation for leaders. They can serve as the prompt leaders need in order to do great things and, in turn, inspire others – creating a virtuous, cross-generational stewardship chain.

Upon joining Unilever as its first outside CEO in 2008 and hearing the story of founder Lord Lever, Paul Polman had a defining moment: "I went back into the origins of Unilever, to discover that [founder] Lord [William] Lever invented the bar soap in Victorian Britain because cholera was such a problem. One of two babies did not make it beyond year one. The problem he tried to solve involved hygiene. In the origins of many companies, people were working in the interests of society, not in the interests of shareholders alone. Focusing only on shareholder value is a very destructive concept."

Through his actions, demonstrating care and empathy for others, Lord Lever had a direct influence on 21st-century Unilever and the Dutch-born, American-educated Polman, who was born over 100 years later. The baton of stewardship passed from generation to generation, steward to steward. Polman discovered that working in the interests of society provides a larger canvas than simply focusing on shareholder value. Driving business in a sustainable way can mean generating sustainable profits.

At Unilever, this legacy translates into long-term investment decisions. While revenue is reported on a quarterly basis, earnings are reported twice per year. This leads to more mature discussions with investors, and longer-term thinking which in turn impacts the company's corporate strategy. It also changes how it views its relationship with shareholders, since in Polman's words, "you have to find shareholders who fit the philosophy of your company." Inspired by the family companies in Asia (where Unilever has a majority of its operations), which aim for higher invested capital and continuous growth, as part of a longer-term strategy, Polman decided to shift his decisions: "to double capital spending, and increase R&D, and [I] did it at the height of a recession when everyone was talking cuts, cuts, cuts. You cannot save your way to prosperity."[2]

Pushed by Polman, the impact of Unilever's sustainability strategy created waves throughout the company. The Unilever Sustainable Living Plan stipulated that Unilever double its turnover while reducing the environmental impact and increasing the social impact. It showed that there was a way to do good and to make money: "We are showcasing a different business model that shows how you give to society and the environment rather than just taking from them," he explained.

Polman has demonstrated commitment and drive, boldly stating his vision to consider the broader and longer-term context when making decisions, and having great influence on stakeholders both inside and outside the company to mobilize around his compelling vision.

Through consistency of action and careful management of resources, Polman has established a reputation for acting with integrity, leading to high levels of trust among Unilever's stakeholders, including consumers, employees, and suppliers.

Stewardship builds a connection with people's hearts and casts a vision of a better future. This pursuit of excellence in capturing values and mind-sets and disseminating them to a new generation of business leaders can also be traced through many of Asia's family-owned and family-run companies. Because the majority of Asian family businesses are still relatively young, there is a limited pool of experience they can draw on when passing the baton to the next generation and handling the challenge that comes with these delicate transitions. Some have been skeptical of governance frameworks, pointing out that key decisions are often made outside these structures. Others have embraced the need to fill the structures with vibrant personalities and activities. They have also realized that vehicles such as charitable foundations, events, publishing, and public speaking represent viable and valuable avenues for articulating and promoting specific sets of family and family business values.[3]

Inspiring with Management Foundations

Many once-great companies have succumbed to hubris and lost their way. These companies fell because they lost sight of what made them great in the first place.

For steward leaders, there are principles that are fundamental and absolute. Great steward leaders hold their beliefs to be true because they have gone through self-contemplation and have proven their convictions to themselves. Such leaders are also transparent about sharing their successes and failures from their unique point of view, and often feel an obligation to inspire stewardship in others.

Some typical areas where steward leaders deliver responsible decision-making include capital structure decisions, liquidity management, and how best to treat employees. These three areas are often fundamental to the way steward leaders view their businesses and the world.

There has been much discussion on whether it is worth borrowing more to increase returns for shareholders and whether it creates or destroys value. Michael Hudson, author of *The Bubble and Beyond*, observed how activist shareholders sometimes push shareholder buybacks for their own benefit, without considering the value destruction effect on the company.[4]

Excessive borrowing can lead to plummeting firm value, hurting creditors and endangering the company. Great steward leaders use less leverage. Borrowing is not regarded as a sensible means of securing long-term greatness. Our empirical results show that companies ranking high on our Implied Stewardship Index have a total debt to total assets ratio of 20.5 percent, while their counterparts, those ranking low on our Implied Stewardship Index, are more leveraged with a total debt to total assets ratio of 29.8 percent. "Good business or investment decisions will eventually produce quite satisfactory economic results, with no aid from leverage," noted Warren Buffett. "It seems to us both foolish and improper to risk what is important (including, necessarily, the welfare of innocent bystanders such as policyholders and employees) for some extra returns that are relatively unimportant."

As part of the measured approach they employ with regard to risk, great steward leaders demonstrate a conservative approach to financing, keeping their companies sufficiently liquid to withstand crisis. "I have pledged – to you, the rating agencies and myself – to always run Berkshire with more than ample cash. We never want to count on the kindness of strangers in order to meet tomorrow's obligations. When forced to choose, I will not trade even a night's sleep for the chance of extra profits," said Warren Buffett.[5] While this may appear overcautious to some, prudence is key to providing stability over time.

On the other side of the globe, Li Ka-shing shared similar views. He observed conservative personal finance practices, always buying land with his own cash, and limiting his stake in any partnership to a minority one and holding no personal debt. He translated these conservative principles to Cheung Kong's corporate practices, and when the company went public in 1972, it had minimal debt. Even in cases when the company needed to borrow, it would buy government bonds amounting to the same amount as the bank loan, to ensure liquidity. The interest income would continue to accumulate, while it repaid interest expense on the loan every month. These conservative financial practices paid off, strengthening the company's ability to withstand shocks. In Li Ka-shing's words: "How many times have you heard that Cheung Kong's finances were in trouble over the last fifty years? Never; the reason is, we are always prepared for the worst."[6]

Strong cash flows had come to the rescue of Li Ka-shing's business empire on several occasions, for instance, in 1982/83 when negotiations on Hong Kong's sovereignty coincided with a global recession and a near-collapse in the property market.[7]

It is interesting to consider the comments of Warren Buffett and Li Ka-shing in light of our study findings. Companies that rank in the upper quartile of our Implied Stewardship Index are more highly liquid than companies ranking in the lower quartile (full details can be found in the Appendix). We compared quick ratios across companies (the quick ratio is a measure of liquidity).[8] The higher the ratio, the better the company's capability to meet current obligations using liquid assets. By being more liquid, companies ranking higher on our Implied Stewardship Index therefore seem better able to absorb the shocks from unanticipated events. Conservative financing helps companies to ensure continuity of their operations and allows them to withstand storms that blow up unexpectedly.

People are central to a firm's continuity, and steward leaders often champion the right of employees to fair treatment. They believe that a culture of caring and respect retains and motivates employees, which is essential to long-term value creation. Pamela Mars-Wright, the great grand-daughter of Franklin C. Mars, who founded Mars in 1911, discussed the central importance she places on the employees, viewing them as family members, and how important it is for her that employees see the company as their legacy. "I walk around a factory and find people who are very proud of what they do ... the best thing in the world is when an associate says this is a great company to work for."[9] Indeed, it is not uncommon for employees to have worked at Mars over two or even three generations, demonstrating how central the company is to their personal lives – and vice versa.

Treating employees as members of the family is quite different from viewing people as a means to profitability. The different kind of connection and bonding creates a deeper level of trust and engagement, building relationships that can endure over time. Steward leaders feel a real responsibility for their employees' well-being, and will do their utmost to ensure they are cared for – even in hard times.

When we look at our Implied Stewardship Index, we notice a clear difference in their approach to downsizing. From 2008 to 2010, during some of the worst years of the financial crisis, companies ranking in the upper quartile of our Implied Stewardship Index downsized

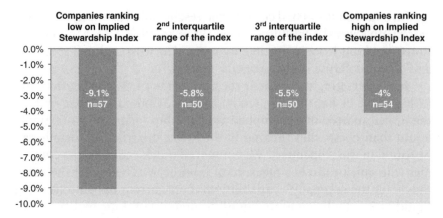

Figure 3.1   Large-scale downsizing by companies ranking low on Implied Stewardship Index versus companies scoring high on Implied Stewardship Index (n=211)

Note: Based on word usage from 870 companies worth more than $10 billion from around the world

less than half as much as those scoring in the lowest quartile (see Figure 3.1).

For Warren Buffett and Li Ka-shing, minimal leverage and high liquidity are parts of their management philosophies; for Pamela Mars-Wright employees are part of the family, a strong foundation of Mars's culture. Both elements are critical to building a company's ability to endure over time and benefit customers and employees alike.

Inspiring with Visionary Thinking

Stewardship is based on the belief that with a firm grounding in prudence and care, as well as passion and purpose, the logic of a firm's trajectory will make sense over time. Even though we have no way of knowing what the future holds, if we act in alignment with our purpose, the course of our trajectory will eventually connect us to the goal we seek to achieve.

In his famous 2005 commencement speech at Stanford, Steve Jobs said: "You can't connect the dots looking forward; you can only connect them looking backwards. So you have to trust that the dots will somehow connect in your future."[10] With the future in mind, great steward leaders think beyond themselves, their organizations, and their lifetime. They think beyond immediate issues, such as remuneration and short-term results. Stewards are able to connect the ordinary with the extraordinary. Today, it is possible to take a broader philosophical view even within some of the previously staunchly technocratic landscapes of global business.

Steward leaders think beyond their compensation package and connect their pay to long-term value creation. Linking C-suite compensation to share prices can lead to market manipulation as executives seek to feather their own nests. In 2013, Equilar reported that more than 60 percent of S&P CEO compensation is in the form of stock. This led Michael Hudson, a research professor, to comment that Equilar, in practice, had been using earnings to give managers stock options. He observed that since managers were incentivized according to how much they could increase the stock price, they would use earnings to push stock up. They would do this, rather than invest in building plant or other more long-term projects, in order to get greater returns from options."[11] What Hudson describes epitomizes short-term, small-picture thinking. In contrast, steward leaders often seem to reach a critical turning point in their success when they are prompted to think bigger, to look beyond their organizations and connect themselves to the larger social good.

Richard Branson describes his personal tipping point: "My business life was running smoothly and my personal life was very happy. Good people were running each of Virgin's 300 companies worldwide. But as I grew older it seemed that I was not making a big enough difference, particularly given my own incredible good fortune. I went from feeling content that things were going well to realizing that I hadn't even begun to scratch the surface of what needed to be done."

Steward leaders have a strong conviction of the need to connect business to a larger purpose, to driving social good. In the words of Richard Branson: "We need a new mind-set to make capitalism an acceptable force in the world. If businesses are purely about profit and amassing bonuses, screwing people and the world in the process, then they will not be around for long, and don't deserve to be."[12]

At the Japanese multinational Fujitsu, the company's objective is not set simply by money making. Behind its brand promise lies its conviction that business operations must look beyond profits, to contribute positively to society. In the face of serious global challenges, including natural disasters, aging populations, food security and environmental issues, Tango Matsumoto, a manager at Fujitsu, described the strong sense of responsibility that imbues the corporate culture and its very reason for being, since "information and communication technology (ICT) companies will have a big role to play in addressing them."[13]

Strongly driven by what will come after them, steward leaders are very focused on their achievements and their legacy. A great deal is at stake – now and in the future. This underlies every decision they make. "In all of our activities, we take a long-term view," said Bill Gates.[14] When Mark Zuckerberg, co-founder of Facebook, was named as one the world's greatest leaders in March 2015 by Fortune, Peter Thiel, a venture capitalist said: "Keeping the company relentlessly focused on the long-term future, he is the opposite of a quarter-to-quarter Wall Street CEO, and that's why he deserves to be recognized as a great leader."[15]

We need to stress here that this is certainly not a common perspective among CEOs. On the contrary, the economic crisis from 2007 to 2009 has been blamed on excessive executive focus on the short term (bank CEOs, in particular, seem to draw the most venom). The topic of short-termism is routinely discussed, debated, and even despised. And yet, the reality is that short-termism is still alive and well.

A 2013 survey of more than 1000 board members and C-suite executives, for example, illustrates that progress toward a longer-term perspective is in many cases slow or non-existent:

- 63 percent of respondents said the pressure to demonstrate short-term financial performance had increased over the previous five years.
- 79 percent felt especially pressured to demonstrate strong financial performance over a period of just two years or less.
- 44 percent said they use a time horizon of less than three years in setting strategy. (73 percent said that a time horizon of more than three years should be used.)
- 86 percent believed that using a longer time horizon to make business decisions would positively affect corporate performance in a number of ways, including strengthening financial returns and increasing innovation.[16]
- Setting strategy with a time horizon of less than three years is unlikely to build something lasting. This is why short-termism is a force for value destruction. In contrast, stewardship is visionary thinking for good. Starting with the bigger picture and broader benefits, great steward leaders inspire with a conviction that others will emulate.

Making Short-term Sacrifices for Long-term Gains

Being willing to absorb short-term pain for a long-term gain is a distinct characteristic of great steward leaders. This may be attributable to hardships in early life, which may serve as an asset in building their capacity to endure short-term sacrifice for long-term reward. Warren Buffett routinely accepts short-term pain. In his opinion, "You shouldn't own common stocks if a 50 percent decrease in their value in a short period of time would cause you acute distress."

With regard to long-term gain, Buffett observes: "When we own portions of outstanding businesses with outstanding managements, our favorite holding period is forever."[17] The logic is simple – short-term pain is an inevitable experience in the route to long-term prosperity. We either suffer the short-term pain of sacrifice and discipline, or the long-term pain of regret. If we have a compelling reason to take action, we will deal with the immediate pain because it is short-term.

When a long-term vision is defined, the decision to endure short-term pain is logical. Consider this episode of the Singapore story, as recounted by Ho Ching, Temasek Holdings' CEO, when she received the 2014 Asian Business Leader's Award: "The newly elected Singapore Government of 1959 soon discovered – to their utter dismay – that they were staring at a budget deficit of some S$14 million for the year. The government kitty had also been emptied by their predecessor government, to the tune of some 10 percent of the island's GDP of a quarter billion pounds. The newly minted Prime Minister (Lee Kuan Yew) and his new Finance Minister went to work with a vengeance. They cut their own salaries by almost a quarter; allowances of top civil servants were also reduced. Projects were shelved. It was an all-out effort and push to reduce the deficit for the year. It was not an easy time. Emotions ran high, as you can imagine, with this unprecedented salary reduction. But, logic and example prevailed, and the civil service pulled together."[18]

By the end of the year, the Finance Minister reported a surplus of S$1 million. This surplus in the first year of self-government set the tone and timbre for fiscal prudence and budget discipline for successive governments to come.

In 1960, GDP per capita in Singapore was a mere $427. In 2013, it was $55,182, one of the highest in Asia. Singapore's leaders managed a miraculous transformation of the country's economy and built the stewardship DNA of the country. As Ho Ching described it: "To live within our means and be financially disciplined; to do the right things with tomorrow clearly in our minds, particularly for our future generations; to make sure that our drive for survival and prosperity go hand in hand with a respect and a nurturing of a clean and green environment for our people."

In the face of adversity, the prospect of long-term benefit provided the sustenance needed to shore up the people of Singapore to forego the path of least resistance in the short term.

Walking Their Talk

Effective steward leaders develop trust through the integrity of their actions and behaviors. By striving for authenticity and consistency in their actions, steward leaders inspire willingness and commitment in others. By understanding the everyday reality of others, they sensitize themselves to the needs of others, communicating with them openly and transparently – often inspiring deep loyalty. Steward leaders walk their talk.

General Wu Qi, 440–381BC, was a Chinese military strategist. According to popular accounts from the time, he was known to take care of his soldiers, and his words and actions were aligned. Records describe him as wearing the same clothes and eating the same food as the most lowly of the soldiers in his army. He was also very attentive to wounded soldiers, ministering to their wounds. When visiting one of his soldiers, he noticed that he had a boil on his skin. The general is reputed to have sucked the pus out of the soldier's boil. Upon hearing the news, the soldier's mother wept. When asked why she was crying, the woman replied; "A few years ago, General Wu Qi did the same thing for the boy's father. My husband was so grateful that he fought and fought until he was killed by the enemy. Now my boy will also die for the general. That is why I'm weeping."[19]

It is difficult to overestimate the commitment this kind of leadership can inspire. General Wu Qi's integrity earned him great trust and loyalty. Soldiers were inspired to go above and beyond their duty, driven by a strong sense of belonging. Inspiration and belonging matter in today's corporations as much as they did in historical armies.

Driving Social Good

Great stewards strive to drive social good through the efforts of the organizations under their leadership. At the organizational level, companies potentially ranking high on stewardship go beyond profitability and consider the interests of all stakeholders. Using the organization as a channel to do good is a vital element of stewardship. Many leaders take this into the personal sphere as well, donating personal or family wealth.

The story of Bill Gates and Microsoft is an often-quoted example. It is typically presented in an entrepreneurial context, focusing on his journey from nothing but vision to creating one of the 20th century's most successful companies. His unwavering dedication to making an impact was even more remarkable.

While many companies make an impact on the community and society indirectly, through initiatives that complement their operations and core business, for Microsoft it was core to its very raison d'être and built into the product itself. The products Microsoft designed and manufactured offered not only superior quality but also scalability. They were platforms that others could build on to create new products, communicate in new ways, and mold their environment to their own image. In the words of Bill Gates: "I think it's fair to say that personal computers have become the most empowering tool we've ever created. They're tools of communication, they're tools of creativity, and they can be shaped by their user."[20]

Bill Gates' description of modern-day leaders as those who empower others has become a popular maxim. And yet this was precisely the thinking that permeated Microsoft's relationship with employees as well as customers and users. Leaving enough space for them to exercise their own talent, curiosity, and creativity – an uncommon proposition at the time among corporate giants and their product development and marketing engines – was always at the heart of the Microsoft philosophy and vision. To quote Bill Gates again: "If you give people tools, and they use their natural ability and their curiosity, they will develop things in ways that will surprise you very much beyond what you might have expected."[21]

But being one of the most successful technology companies globally, sustaining consistent performance over three decades, was not enough for Gates. In 1993, he visited Africa for the first time. He was disturbed by the fact that millions of children were dying from diseases like measles, hepatitis B, yellow fever, and rotavirus. "That was deeply upsetting … I became convinced that if science and technology were better applied to the challenges of Africa, the tremendous potential of the continent would be unleashed and people could be healthier and fulfil their promise."

Gates began giving his money away in 1994, and in 2000, Bill and Melinda Gates launched their foundation to enhance healthcare, reduce extreme poverty globally, and expand educational opportunities and access to information technology (in the United States specifically). As of May 16, 2013, Bill Gates had donated $28 billion to the Foundation, which had a total endowment of $42.3 billion in 2014. Not content with simply giving, the Foundation seeks to maximize its impact. With a guiding philosophy of actionable measurement, the Foundation places great emphasis on evaluation as instrumental in helping to guide effective decision-making by providing objective data that can inform action.

Gates mentioned that his motivation to address health and education was that these were market failures, i.e., areas where capitalism had fallen short.[22] Through his clear and ongoing commitment to helping solve intractable problems of health and education, as well as the undoubtable business impact that Microsoft has had, Gates clearly demonstrates the qualities of stewardship.

In 2006, Warren Buffett, then the world's richest person, pledged to commit his wealth to the Gates Foundation. The joint effort doubled the Foundation's annual giving. Since inception, the Gates Foundation's overall grant payments total $32.9 billion (as of December 31, 2014).

In 2009, during a dinner organized by the Foundation, Marguerite Lenfest (wife of media entrepreneur and philanthropist H.F. Lenfest) proposed that the rich should sit down, decide how much money they and their progeny need, and figure out what to do with the rest of it. This was the start of the Giving Pledge. In 2010, the campaign was formally announced. Warren Buffett and Bill Gates began convincing billionaires around the globe to give half their wealth to philanthropy.

By the end of 2014, 129 of the world's wealthiest individuals and families had dedicated the majority of their wealth to philanthropy. Great steward leaders think alike. Participating in good deeds inspires more and more steward leaders to join forces. The Giving Pledge aims to help achieve the following:

- "Inspire conversations, discussions, and action, not just about how much but also for what purposes/to what end"; and,
- "Bring together those committed to this kind of giving to exchange knowledge on how to do this in the best possible way."[23]

The inspiration of the Giving Pledge goes beyond "how much," "to what end", and "how to." It also inspires people to give away earlier in their lives. "We have heard from pledgers that they have been inspired to start giving away more, earlier in their lives," said Melinda Gates, co-chair of the Gates Foundation. "The opportunity to learn from one another's successes and failures is helping us become better philanthropists and maximizing the impact of our giving."[24]

Doing good contributes to building an inspiring context and influences the overall tone of a company's view of itself in the world. An impressive qualitative difference in tone of their communication is demonstrated by our study findings. Words like *achieve, boost, driven, embrace, enriching, fun, good, improve, progress, stable, strong*, and *successful* are used by potentially well-stewarded companies, compared with *bad, cancel, failed, ineffectiveness, lack, limitation,* and *stress* used by potentially poorly stewarded companies (see Appendix for more details). In consciously having positive impacts for the world, great steward leaders inspire other stewards and individuals to make the choices that will push such impacts forward, multiplying the effects over time and contexts.

Communicating Passionately

Great steward leaders are articulate and passionate in communicating about stewardship. Passion stirs curiosity and prompts others to wonder what drives great steward leaders. Passionate communication might not be a prerequisite condition of a great steward. Yet transparency and openness characterize how great steward leaders communicate with stakeholders.

While not all steward leaders are born communicators, they recognize how important it is to get their ideas across effectively – and put in the effort to raise their game in this area.

Warren Buffett was probably Dale Carnegie's most influential graduate.[25] "I was terrified of public speaking. You can't believe what I was like if I had to give a talk. I was so terrified that I just couldn't do it. I would throw up. In fact, I arranged my life so that I never had to get up in front of anybody," Buffett said.[26] He enrolled in a public speaking course but dropped out before it started. At the age of 21, Buffett decided that to reach the audiences to whom he needed to convey his message, he had to overcome his fear of public speaking. He describes it as follows: "When I came out here to Omaha after graduating, I saw another ad. And I knew I was going to have to speak in public sometimes. The agony was such that just to get rid of the pain I signed up for the course again ... There were about twenty-five or thirty of us in there. We were all just terrified. We couldn't say our own names. We all stood there and wouldn't talk to each other."[27]

The public speaking course worked for Buffett. When he was asked what habits built the foundation of his success, Buffett stressed the importance of communication: "You've got to be able to communicate in life and it's enormously important. Schools, to some extent, under-emphasize that. If you can't communicate and talk to other people and get across your ideas, you're giving up your potential."[28]

Steward leaders consciously communicate their passionate vision, taking advantage of the array of available platforms: books, forums, conferences, presentations, talks, TV shows, and interviews. In a world where content is freely available online, they make sure to get their message across in a consistent manner.

The proliferation of online media platforms also means that those messages can be accessed by growing numbers of people in increasingly far-flung locations. A search for Bill Gates on YouTube, for example, yields around 2.95 million results. By crossing boundaries of geography, education, and social context in a way the world has never seen before, their messages may reach unanticipated audiences and spark a shift in thinking that may alter the direction of many lives. By enhancing the awareness of our increasing connection and ability to effect change in the world, steward leaders move us to contribute the best of ourselves to do our part.

PART II

WHAT DRIVES STEWARDSHIP?

CHAPTER

4

Stewardship Values and Beliefs

Whether clearly defined or hidden from view, values and beliefs are at the core of our activity and form the basis of our decisions. They are the bedrock of individual lives as well as organizations. And they are the foundations of stewardship.

Because values express a guiding truth, in day-to-day situations they are acted on, even instinctively, rather than observed. Ratan Tata expressed it this way: "Apart from values and ethics which I have tried to live by, the legacy I would like to leave behind is a very simple one – that I have always stood up for what I consider to be the right thing, and I have tried to be as fair and equitable as I could be."

In fact, values are by definition stable and enduring, such that most people will seldom need to articulate or try to clarify them, unless they come across a visible contradiction or threat.[1]

At the heart of many values and beliefs is a simple question: What does it mean to be human in this world? Stewardship asks a similar question of organizations: What does it mean to run a business in today's world?

It is difficult to answer without pointing to the need for a strong sense of values to sustain an organization against any change in business environment. Indeed, it is values rather than incentives that motivate the actions of true leaders. As Eiji Toyoda observed: "Doing the right things, when required, is a calling from on high. Do it boldly, do as you believe, do as you are."[2]

Safeguarding, promoting, and actively acting on an organization's values allow its leaders (owners, board, and management) to act as stewards. This is because values underpin and frame the company's motivation to create long-term benefits, not only for shareholders but for all of society. The following sections describe the main types of values manifested by steward leaders and organizations around the world, and notably in Asia.

Enlightened Leadership

Fundamentally, stewardship is an enlightened form of business leadership. It is concerned not only with generating returns on investments but also with guiding a business onto a path of sustained success. It gives owners and managers a powerful sense of attachment and responsibility to their entire community. In its most natural state, this ownership mentality can be found among founder-owners and family-owned companies. But it can also be nurtured in other groups of steward leaders, and ultimately shape their view of business as a force for good. Stewardship is a force that restores business to its rightful place in society.

Companies that are driven by this ownership mind-set, and whose values are evident in their day-to-day operations, are in a good position to provide their leaders and employees alike with clarity of purpose. Drawing on this clearly felt meaning and purpose, their employees develop a sense of belonging. In fact, much of their individual and group identity becomes rooted in their work. It allows them to enact this purpose as they go about meeting goals and targets. More importantly, it helps them reflect on and make sense of their workplace experiences. This, in turn, reassures them about who they are and what they stand for.[3]

The vision of stewardship and its theoretical underpinnings are hardly new. Thought leaders like Henry Mintzberg noted many years ago that the essence of management was synthesis rather than analysis. Without adopting the term "steward," Mintzberg put forward the ideal of a manager who was committed to a specific company or industry, and not to management as a means of personal advancement. Similarly, the late management scholar Sumantra Ghoshal spoke of management as "a calling and a profession that sits at the heart of creating good for society and for individuals. ... So many senior managers care deeply about their role in society. They are trying to do the best they can for the good of the world. My interest in these issues flows out of their aspirations and their efforts."[4]

Throughout history, Asian societies have subscribed to what philosophers have termed a "this world" way of thinking. They have sought meaning in the specific rather than the abstract, avoiding the neat dualities of public vs. private, professional vs. personal, business vs. non-business, which are common in the West. While Platonic dualism (which forms much of Western thought) is based on the dualism of the mind–body split (whereby the body is subordinate to the intellectual) and the subject–object split (whereby the self is defined in opposition to the Other, i.e., other human beings or nature), non-dualism emphasizes that we are whole beings, inextricably and fundamentally interconnected to each other and to the physical world, as of rather than in the world.[5]

It is not surprising, then, that many of Asia's leading companies embraced a mind-set of doing good very early on in their existence. The leaders of India's Tata group, for instance, have promoted their understanding that business cannot operate independently of social, geopolitical, environmental, and human needs, but must balance these diverse needs. They defined their company's core purpose as improving the quality of life of the communities it serves globally. The company's founder Jamsetji Tata (1839–1904) stated it right from the outset: "In a free enterprise, the community is not just another stakeholder in business, but is in fact the very purpose of its existence."[6]

Half a century later, Japan's Konosuke Matsushita firmly believed that a business as large as his was responsible for helping all of society to prosper. The principles he popularized as "Matsushita's seven spirits" embraced ideas virtually unheard of in business in his day.

Matsushita's views resonate with those of other leaders including Acer's Stan Shih, who wrote: "For an entrepreneur, a core question is 'Why should a particular enterprise exist?'" In Shih's view, a company's contribution to society should be the foundation of its reason for being, since it relies on societal health for its own goals. Therefore, in Shih's words, "If a company is concerned only with its own demands, benefits, and financial returns, it deviates from its basic values."[7] Indeed, companies which could not contribute to society should not exist.

The good of the organization, company, or country under steward leadership will trump any personal considerations or aspirations. When Lee Kuan Yew of Singapore proclaimed in an interview, "Even from my sick bed, even if you are going to lower me into the grave, and I feel something is going wrong, I will get up," he verbalized the passion and ownership mentality attached to a work painstakingly built up through effort. This sentiment is shared by many business and political leaders who are founder-owners or who strongly identify with their work. Many such modern-day business leaders have expressed a similar desire to ensure that their company not only survives but also creates impetus for social, cultural, and economic change.

In the words of Ayala Corporation's Jaime Zóbel de Ayala: "We believe that visionary companies seek profits but they are equally guided by a core ideology, core values and a sense of purpose beyond just making money."[8]

Today, these beliefs reverberate as strongly as ever. Around the world, companies have worked to strengthen the well-being of communities wherever they have invested.

In addition to having a clear sense of ownership and purpose, and engaging various stakeholders in society, a long-term horizon for evaluating a company's business is another key dimension of the stewardship approach. It builds on the awareness that leaders are but temporary custodians.

Our study findings highlight how this view translates into investment in long-term capabilities, for example when we look at investment in R&D. When we examine investment in R&D as a percentage of sales, there is a clear difference between companies. Companies ranking in the top quartile of the Implied Stewardship Index invest a significantly higher percentage of their revenues in R&D, compare to those ranking in the lowest quartile, as can be seen in Figure 4.1. This investment contributes to building their competitive and innovative capability for the long term.

This long-term view is reinforced by a notion that the assets in their care must be protected over a time frame that exceeds any individual owner's or manager's tenure. In many ways, it is the direct opposite of the chronic "short-termism" of much modern-day business management. It takes a wider view that goes far beyond merely complying with the requirements of corporate governance or creating short-term shareholder benefits.

Among Asian companies, there is a similar trend to benchmark their impact on social good against global development and sustainability objectives. Hong Kong's Li & Fung, for example, publishes an annual Communication on Progress to document the steps it has taken in embracing global sustainability principles. In this report, the

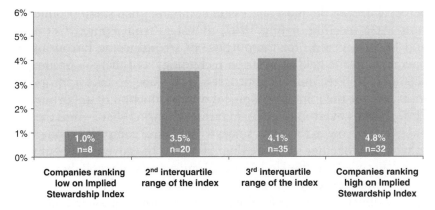

Figure 4.1   Investment in R&D (percent of sales) (2009–2014)

company defines its understanding of what it means to operate a sustainable business: namely, one that provides goods and services that create value, creates jobs, has transparency and integrity in its operations, has efficient use of resources and a concern for environmental protection. In this way, business acts as an important contributor to society over time: "Over the long term, such a business will make major contributions to the social and economic well-being of the communities in which it operates."[9]

Serving the Nation

What motivates this long-term view of business success and its impact on society? In developing societies that share a painful history of colonial rule and wartime occupation, followed by national independence and its new economic agenda, a surprising number of business leaders point to a love for their country, or even "nationalism," with no negative connotations. This identification with the nation state may be more relevant for stewardship in contexts where institutional gaps are more prevalent. The largest aerospace and defense company in Europe, Airbus, was established to promote European industry. In joining forces, Germany, France, and the United Kingdom sought to promote economic goals over the long term in order to compete with the United States in aerospace. Between 1958 and 1985, American firms had 83 percent market share – with Boeing owning the biggest piece of the pie. Despite considerable European expertise in aerospace, even the most successful companies had small production runs. At a meeting in July 1967, ministers from France, Germany, and Britain agreed "for the purpose of strengthening European cooperation in the field of aviation technology and thereby promoting economic and technological progress in Europe, to take appropriate measures for the joint development and production of an airbus." In 2002, Airbus overtook Boeing in terms of market share – and the gap has been narrow in the years since, with intense competition ongoing. In working together for more than 30 years, the governments of Germany, France, and the United Kingdom successfully collaborated to achieve positive economic impact, with clear societal benefits (including job creation and technological innovation) for their countries' citizens.

In South Korea, Lee Byung-chul founded Samsung group around a set of key principles. The first was economic contribution to the nation (the other two were prioritizing human resources and adopting an approach of rationality).[10] Similarly, the leaders of Taiwan's technology industry have been actively helping to brand Taiwan Inc.

In India, companies like Infosys have been at the forefront of a new India Inc. since the early 1980s. Ayala Corporation has had over 160 years of history that was closely linked to the story of the Philippines. The current generation of leadership is keen to continue building on their ancestors' vision of being a "catalyst for growth and entrepreneurial development" in the country. To quote Canon's Fujio Mitarai: "People's love of country is one of the most important sentiments that should be fostered from childhood as the spiritual foundation of members of society or citizens of the world."[11]

Similarly, Tata group's publicly stated values include not only faith and reliability but also service to the nation. From its inception, which predates the country's independence, Tata's focus was on "foundation industries" that would contribute to making the country self-sufficient and industrialized.[12] This was passed down with the leadership succession. By the time Ratan Tata took over the leadership of the company, he had a broad and optimistic vision for India. In his words: "I am proud of my country. But we need to unite to make a unified India, free of communalism and casteism. We need to build India into a land of equal opportunity for all. We can be a truly great nation if we set our sights high and deliver to the people the fruits of continued growth, prosperity and equal opportunity."[13]

These sentiments are echoed by Wipro's Azim Premji: "There is noteworthy effort from most of the corporate leaders to go beyond our business constituency and influence the issues that matter most to our country."[14]

In 2008, president director of the state-owned Indonesia Port Corporation (IPC), Richard J. Lino, known as "Pak Lino," returned to the company after 20 years in the private sector. On the list of company values put forward by Pak Lino upon his return to IPC, "nationalism" was ranked near the top, right behind "not [being] afraid of change." He commented: "What motivated me to take over the transformation of a slow-moving, government-run company? Personally, it is not about money or glory. I want to contribute. Ever since I was a child, I was thinking about the sea that surrounds us and how one day this may allow me to do something for my country."[15]

While identifying with a broader context than one's individual unit (such as the nation state) may prompt greater stewardship (in terms of considering the good of society), we would like to stress that this is not always the case – especially when national ends are pursued over and above the global good, for example leading to trade protectionism or geopolitical conflict. This may be exacerbated in cultural contexts where collectivism is relatively preferred over individualism – depending on the type of collectivism (as we saw in Chapter 2).

In the Asian context, there is a greater relative preference for collectivism – which often involves extended family – and the nation state. Thus cultural inclination may contribute to building a foundation for anticipating and rewarding stewardship behavior. The importance attached to collectivism in many Asian societies is also a natural reflection of the emphasis given to teamwork and the tendency to engage employees at an emotional level. Collectivism can be a powerful agent in promoting stewardship in the national context. However, when taken to an extreme, it can be counter-productive for stewardship.

Trust Opens the Door to Stewardship

Another way for organizational leaders to strengthen employees' sense of personal ownership and open the door to stewardship action is by building an atmosphere of reciprocity and trust. A sense of trust is critical in that it gives employees the secure base they need in order to take risks and innovate. As noted by Hyundai's Chung Ju-yung: "The most valuable asset for bringing progress to society is its people. Capital, material resources and technology are all secondary."[16] In the early 1980s, the company articulated diligence, frugality, and love as the corporation's core values. In this spirit, Chung practiced the philosophy of *samgo choyeo*, or inviting talented people to do their work patiently before granting them authority and responsibility.

Employees in an organization are seen as members of a family. The organization's leader is expected to accept personal responsibility for their well-being. To exercise effective leadership then means to downplay the sense of self and focus on relationships and context.

What is interesting about the trust equation is that many communication styles and personality traits that are common in Asian cultures have, over the years, found their way into local organizational behavior. For instance, Japanese leaders are known to suggest indirect, often non-specific instructions and guidelines to their subordinates for business projects, demonstrating a sense of trust in the workers' ability. Likewise, compliments, rewards, and criticism in a business setting are shared collectively by team members in order to maintain the status quo of fairness. Indonesian culture traditionally values conformism, humility, and conflict avoidance, so openly aiming for high visibility and success is often frowned upon. Trust is typically invested in kinship and family ties, and in relationships based on patronage. As a result, employees in Indonesia retain a preference for informal, vaguely defined relationships and leadership styles.

In an effort to cultivate team spirit, Taiwan's Acer stresses a mission shared by all employees in a "family-like" business. To quote Acer's founder Stan Shih: "We valued the benefits of 'family' and interpreted our company in a different way (although still Eastern) by using the term 'business family.'"[17]

The awareness of the needs of others is what helped Stan Shih nurture this familial atmosphere: "I for one believe that helping others is the best way to help yourself. Although the connection is indirect, it's sustainable. That's my winning strategy. In the past, control [was about] who owns 51 percent of the company. It makes much more sense to control a company by managing the common interest of the people inside of it."[18]

Shih's ability to understand his strengths and weaknesses helped him to stay in an inquiry mode, always questioning his role and taking responsibility in the event of a crisis: "When something goes wrong a leader always asks 'what's wrong with me,' not 'what's wrong with them.'"

This was an important element of his strong contextual awareness, understanding employees' needs for autonomy to feel motivated. Shih was acutely aware of the fact that organizations depended on people for their success – and continuously strived to motivate them and build their individual ability to contribute – as well as to enhance their desire to do so. He recognized that this was a different starting point from many other companies, which aim to control their employees, with a view to preventing corruption and opportunism. In contrast, Shih said: "I place full confidence in my employees and allow them great discretion in their daily work life."[19]

The difference in narrative related to people and processes by potentially well-stewarded companies reflects this care. When considering the results of our word content analysis, the difference in terms used in relation to people and processes is powerful. Companies potentially ranking high on stewardship use words such as *engaged*, *dynamic*, *promote*, *talent*, and *expertise*, indicative of the lens through which they view their people (see Table 4.1).

Striving to be Invisible

Leading visibly from the front may be common in Western societies, but less so in other parts of the world. The notion of saving face is significant in many Asian cultures, especially the Chinese. When a leader is criticized or challenged publicly, such direct confrontation or failure to show respect results in loss of face. To avoid such a consequence, this often leads to a tendency to suppress negative opinions

Table 4.1   Differences in word usage related to people and processes

Companies potentially ranking high on stewardship	Companies potentially ranking low on stewardship
career, colleagues, commitment, compensation, diversity, employee, empower, engaged, expertise, grooming, individual, people, performance, promote, recognize, recruitment, reward, safety, spirit, staff, talent, team.	appraisal, assigned, compensatory, dismiss, evaluated, hire, job, nonqualified, payroll, postretirement, qualifying, replaced, replacement, retention, uncommitted, unemployment, wage.

and emotions. A result of this is the "invisible leadership" in the classical Chinese mold and "gently leading by the hand" in Southeast Asian cultures.

Drawing inspiration from ancient Chinese philosophy, some business leaders have found a source of energy for reinvigorating their business in the style of "invisible leadership" (which gives staff ample room for making decisions and taking the initiative) and "always considering the well-being of others." The fourth generation of Lee Kum Kee's owners has adapted these to the metaphors of "auto-pilot leadership model" and "helicopter view." The Lee brothers have established themselves as noted authors, speakers, and experts on applying tenets of Chinese tradition to achieving success in modern-day life and business.

Nurturing a sense of group harmony in the workforce is crucial to forging emotional bonds among employees and between employees and the company. For decades, promoting a sense of organizational belonging and group culture was one of the essential management tools in many Korean companies. It is common for staff across different levels of the organization's hierarchy to meet frequently after work for meals, drinking, singing, and visiting homes. Since relationships are often more important than rules, embracing this social aspect of one's job is critical to accessing job prospects and for a person's future with the company.

In the past, Samsung Electronics implemented a team-focused campaign entitled "My machine, my area, my job." It involved setting team-level performance goals for major groups across the organization, and at the same time defining more detailed individual responsibilities and roles that would directly contribute to achieving team-level objectives. The program dramatically improved the sense of ownership and motivation among individuals, while maintaining a clear sense of team mission and empowerment.[20] Its combination of autonomy and connection to a meaningful collective purpose helped to cultivate the employees' intrinsic motivation.

For his part, Hyundai's founder Chung Ju-yung had faith in the intelligence and diligence of his workers, holding that Korean human resources are second to none. His approach was to invite talented people to prove themselves through good work before promoting them. Chung's approach was reflected in the core values still held by Hyundai and implemented by a management policy based on trust.

Trust also inspired Zhang Ruimin, founder and chairman of China's Haier Group, to steer the company organization toward participative management, decentralized decision-making, and autonomous but accountable work teams and platforms. He built a workforce of 80,000 who were empowered to work in self-organizing, autonomous work units.[21]

A 2013 report on Haier discussed how the old-economy, commodity-type player reinvented itself by "embracing the contradictions of being simultaneously structured yet entrepreneurial, disciplined yet flexible, and tactical yet strategic." It also described Zhang Ruimin's visionary leadership as "unreasonable and inspiring at the same time."[22] Today, Zhang continues to distribute authority across the organization, down to frontline staff, thus creating an atmosphere of invisible leadership and management without bosses.

The Handover

One of the hallmarks of well-stewarded companies is that they balance their actions to benefit and sustain not only the present generation but also future ones. This comes from a deeply-held understanding and conviction that casts business leaders as custodians, as stewards.

As attached as they are to their organizations, and as much as they desire to guide them onto a path of sustained success, in the grand scheme of things their mandate is only temporary and will one day expire. Therefore, as trusted and responsible stewards, they (owner, board, and management) seek to be able to hand over a thriving business and organization – in better shape than what they themselves took over when they assumed their roles – to the next generation or to their successors.

This dimension can often be seen in family businesses, many of which are focused on sustaining and perpetuating their business for the long term due to a sense of responsibility for the well-being of their parents' business legacy. Another key characteristic of family firms that lends itself well to stewardship, particularly in Asia, is the relative absence of clear dividing lines between family and community, business and society. In fact, having to choose between personal and professional relationships in a family business has traditionally been considered awkward and painful, and best avoided altogether. Nonetheless, every family business is different. Some research studies have paid attention to the degree to which a business is embedded within the owner family (e.g., number of generations, family directors, managers). Their findings suggest that high levels of this type of embeddedness serve as an obstacle to greater adoption of stewardship behavior.[23]

Acknowledging the family to be larger and ultimately more important than the business, e.g., by adopting an "enterprising family" management model, has helped a number of successful family businesses improve their focus on engaging the next generation of owners.

After years of channeling its philanthropic activities through the company's business divisions, the owners of Lee Kum Kee International Holdings established the Lee Kum Kee Family Foundation. It is dedicated to advocating family solidarity and strengthening effective communication in multi-generational families. By working with low-income families in Hong Kong and South China and involving them in "loving family" learning platforms, the Lee family has made improvements in its own communications that target multiple generations of the family. As one of the family leaders puts it: "We create positive examples and leave people feeling touched so that they want to come back. So far, all stakeholders want us to continue, including external partners and the government."[24]

Much of Lee Kum Kee's success in navigation and growth in an ever-changing and increasingly complex business as well as social and political environment could be attributed to the fourth generation's decision, some 10 to 15 years earlier, to assume big-picture roles in the organization. In many family companies experiencing fast growth and diversification, the new generation of owners might instinctively follow the opposite route and get bogged down in day-to-day responsibilities. The new cohort of Lee Kum Kee's owners not only knew better but also realized early on that their main mission included:

- Creating and maintaining structures and processes that would readily support the family and the business as they grew and evolved;
- Imbuing these structures with the family's and the family company's values;
- Sparing no time and effort in articulating, nurturing and promoting these values within the family as well as in the outside world.

Staying True to Tradition

The fortunes of other family-owned companies such as Singapore's Eu Yan Sang, a retailer of traditional Chinese herbal and medicinal products, have also been on the upswing. Eu Yan Sang has made great strides over the past few years by healing family conflicts; revitalizing a 130-year-old brand; and ramping up domestic and international sales. French family business Bel combined traditional local recipes with modern marketing and production to become a world leader in branded cheeses. Led by Antoine Fiévet, a descendant of founder Léon Bel, Bel built upon its 150-year history and its strong values to re-invent itself over five generations. It prides itself on its ongoing governance dialogue within the family, constantly challenging its assumptions to adapt to changing environments in pursuit of the most efficient balance between family and business forces. These examples provide a good illustration of steward leaders' long-term orientation, which provides for strong company and organizational continuity.

Steward leaders who have a clear view of their firm's purpose are in a good position to reinforce this continuity by embracing values and beliefs that are specific to their culture and tradition. Instead of setting aside traditional values as a distraction from universal theories and practices of management, they recognize that these values can be fitted into a leadership framework that will ultimately strengthen business performance.

Across Southeast Asia, the traditions of immigrant communities and their rags-to-riches stories have shaped local attitudes to business and its place in society. The majority of immigrants who arrived from China in the late 19th and early 20th centuries were contract workers and miners, or farmers and fishermen from rural backgrounds. Later on, some of them settled into merchant roles. Historically, Chinese society had low social respect for trade. Hence, in the new overseas setting, trading, business, and money itself had to be reinvented, redefined, and upheld by the newly arrived immigrants.

Today, their industriousness lives on, most visibly in Singapore's "no free lunch" work ethic. For his part, India's J.R.D. Tata, who led the Tata group over a period of more than 50 years, from 1938 to 1991, expressed a similar idea when he said: "Nothing worthwhile is ever achieved without deep thought and hard work."[25] In these and in other countries, steward leaders have had to draw on their resourcefulness, in the process demonstrating great drive, passion, and commitment to creating a better reality. Their ability to channel their remarkable energy reserves scarcely wavered over time.

But not all the values propagated by migrant workers from South China and other parts of Asia had to do with money and trading. On the contrary, they included seeking out formal and informal opportunities to learn; learning by doing; familial solidarity; and a sense of frugality. The migrants demonstrated a tremendous willingness to examine their strengths and weaknesses; to listen to and learn from others; and to question the validity of their own assumptions in the new environment.

Fast-forward to 2015 when many visitors to online discussion forums have commented that they were "stunned" when visiting the unassuming offices – even compared with local government offices – of Indonesia's leading consumer brand StandardPen (owned by the ethnic Chinese Susanto family), a company with a strong reputation and high volume of international sales. But it is this simplicity, work ethic, and unerring focus on results rather than appearances that has anchored the owners' and their ancestors' experience as migrant entrepreneurs in an adopted homeland.

To quote J.R.D. Tata again: "Companies need to save up for the future so that when the opportunity arises they can make bold investments in new business undertakings. This, of course, requires the kind of frugality that takes every sensible measure to save on a daily basis. This kind of self-imposed frugality and economy also helps to foster a serious attitude toward one's work and a desire to produce fine goods or services."[26]

Steward leaders understand well that it is important to take a step back and ask what leadership really means in the context of their specific cultural, institutional, and business environments and historical circumstances. Without deep thought about what it represents to their organizations and how these organizations can best absorb, internalize, and act on it, talking about leadership will amount to little more than window dressing. Through understanding the wider ramifications of what is required of them and their organizations, stewards draw upon their contextual awareness to inform their decision-making.

Alibaba's founder Jack Ma, for example, owes much of his success to understanding that in China, every transaction is personal. Moreover, he realized that culture, history, philosophy, and mind-set were as important as functionality when adapting technological concepts specifically for China. That is also the reason he included a real-time chat function on the online auction website *Taobao*, so that buyers and sellers could build a relationship and trust and negotiate in real time.

Speaking about the aspirations of the Chinese people, Acer founder Stan Shih felt strongly that the Chinese should seize the opportunity for a second industrial revolution to boost economic power on the international stage. He became increasingly convinced that Chinese expertise would enable the region to become a center of expertise in the high-tech sector. In 1986 – 10 years after founding Acer – young, educated people were remaining overseas after completing advanced studies. Shih decided to try to help "Chinese Dreams Come True," – building a dream for young people by creating exciting job opportunities in Taiwan. After discovering the potential of microprocessors, Shih and his partners set a mission for Acer, "as the 'gardener of the microprocessor' to make the microprocessor technologies available to all."[27]

The Steward State

The paths to building stewardship in different societies have to be inclusive and pluralistic. There is truly no one-size-fits-all approach. This becomes evident when examining the role of governments and state-owned enterprises in the stewardship space. It would be unrealistic to expect China, for instance, amid the country's momentous and ongoing transformation from a state-controlled, command system to a market that drives the global economy, to fit into a "universal" stewardship model.

The bigger picture of China's reforms shows a landscape of young and fast-growing state-owned enterprises negotiating a steep learning curve. Over the past 10 to 20 years, they have evolved and modernized at varying rates. Many are run by former political cadres, or may see their current leaders accept political roles in central and provincial governments. Some have learned difficult lessons from their past when searching for and defining clear boundaries – previously non-existent – between ownership and management, business and politics, corporate roles and party mandates.

As they develop, these enterprises are fulfilling the central government's mandate by embarking on aggressive internationalization and a spate of worldwide acquisitions. In the process, they are studying best practices from many different business environments, both in developed and developing markets.

The overarching objective is explained by Bank of China governor Zhou Xiaochuan: "To support a sound and sustained development of the economy and contribute to the realization of the Chinese dream of great rejuvenation of the Chinese nation."[28] Likewise, Zhang Jianguo, China Construction Bank CEO, explained that the state-owned lender has to fulfill its social responsibility according to central government policy: "We loan to small and medium-sized businesses, to the rural economy, to the coastal cities, to the middle of China, to the North East and the West."[29]

In its early days of national independence, following its split with the Malaysian federation, Singapore likewise tapped its corporate sector for talent, resources, and expertise. These were applied toward building the economy for an island faced with the reality of no natural resources, scarcity of land, and limited manpower. When the Development Bank of Singapore (DBS) was established in 1968, its main functions were to provide loans to Singapore's manufacturing sector; to assist in establishing new industries and upgrading existing ones; to support projects from the Urban Renewal Program; and to facilitate tourism initiatives.

At about the same time, within a few years of independence, Singapore government-linked companies like Keppel Corporation started providing training programs to develop local industry, overcome the lack of manpower, and offer career prospects to national servicemen re-entering civilian life. Other business and government-linked organizations also contributed in various ways to Singapore's nation-building effort. For instance, during the financial crisis of 1997, the Singapore government offered every citizen the opportunity to buy 500 shares of SingTel at 26 percent below their market price. It also offered additional "loyalty shares" to citizens who would hold on to their allotment.[30]

There are many other examples of governments getting involved in the business sector to act as stewards, ensuring citizens are able to reap the rewards that may not always be available to them, and building societal connections with enterprises. For example, in 1993 the French government sold six million shares of chemical company Rhône-Poulenc. The offering was well received – oversubscribed by a factor of four. By the end of the year, nearly three million people had become new shareholders, with employees holding 6 percent of the company's capital.

CHAPTER 5

Personality Traits and Attitudes of Steward Leaders

Values and beliefs are the bedrock of stewardship. To them are added the usual complexities of human personalities and individuality, the bewildering powers of nature and nurture, character and circumstance. Making sense of these is a vital ingredient in better understanding stewardship and the nature of steward leaders.

The way that the personalities of great leaders are examined has evolved dramatically in recent decades[1,2] (see Figure 5.1). Early theories on the personality aspects of leadership are described as "great man" theories. They presented leaders – who were almost exclusively male – as heroic, mythical, and uniquely destined to rise to leadership as and when their skills were needed.[3]

This paradigm gradually gave way to the realization that great leadership is not always rooted in heroic archetypes, or characterized by qualities traditionally regarded as male, or even limited to the highest echelons of power. This understanding spurred psychologists and leadership experts to observe, describe, and classify specific attributes of personality and character shared by successful, effective leaders. Increasingly, these observations took place in a business environment as well, as opposed to the traditional settings of politics and the military.

These personality- and trait-based approaches to leadership continue to be popular and productive. As a result, every few months a

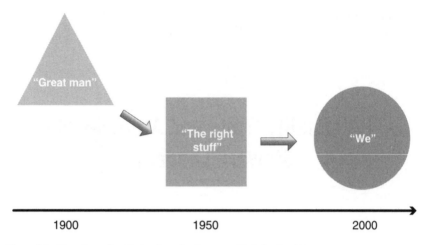

Figure 5.1   A century of analyzing the role of personality in leadership
Adapted from: Bligh, M. (2010),[4] Haslam, et al. (2011)[5]

new, catchy list appears of the latest top five qualities that have been recognized as essential to great leadership. This is the "right stuff" one must possess in order to have the chance of growing into a true leader. Meanwhile, the popularization of terms like "emotional intelligence" and "charisma" in management has both reinforced and blurred the concept of individual personality traits as key building blocks of effective leaders and leadership.

Personality- and trait-based analyses of great leadership are not without their detractors, who suggest this perspective limits itself to the tools, jargon, and imagery of elementary psychology. Yet there is no denying that, as IMD professor George Kohlrieser puts it, responsible leadership "starts with the leader as a person – his or her integrity, values, mission, personality and life experiences."[6]

In recent years, a more integrated approach has emerged. This aims to step away from viewing leaders in isolation, and to explore the interactions they enter into with their followers, as well as the effect they produce in them. Some researchers have fittingly labeled this trend as analyzing the "willingness to identify as a 'we.'" According to this approach, no fixed set of personality traits can assure good leadership because the most desirable traits depend on the nature of the group being led.[7]

Men and Supermen

If we look at the cast of steward leaders we introduced in Chapter 1, some are indeed "near-mythical," venerated individuals wholly deserving of the "great man" honorific.

Take Hyundai's supremely self-confident leader Chung Ju-yung who titled his autobiography *Many Trials, No Failures*. His company's focus on construction and shipbuilding in many ways mirrored the emphasis that Korean society traditionally placed – and continues to place – on male, aggressive qualities and character traits.

In the past, male trainees at Hyundai's companies were expected to build up their stamina through physical exercise and sometimes marched in military formations before the start of their work shift.[8] Chung proudly relied predominantly on Korean technology and know-how, even when venturing into untested areas such as shipbuilding. In his opinion, Korean human resources were outstanding. Speaking of Hyundai's first automobiles, he said: "Cars are like national flags with wheels. If we make good cars and export them, they drive around the world, spreading Korea's technology and level of industrialization."[9]

The stories of other steward leaders involve less of the superman element. Rather, they build on the presence of strong character traits. In all cases, it was crucial to the leaders' success that they connected with and galvanized their followers at make-or-break points in their organizations' and societies' history.

A powerful recurring theme is the adversity the leaders had to overcome in breaking out of poverty and a pervasive lack of opportunity. Chung Ju-yung was born and raised in today's North Korea to an impoverished rural family as the eldest of six children. By the age of 15, he was a married man – not uncommon in his community at the time. Still only a teenager, he hatched several plans to escape to the nearby city and work in low-paid construction and factory jobs.

Similarly, Acer's Stan Shih remembers being an introverted child who worked throughout his primary school years in his mother's business in order to help support the family.

Konosuke Matsushita was born into a once well-to-do farming family that had lost its fortune. Three of his elder siblings died in childhood and he only received education until the age of nine. In fact, many chapters in his life story were tragic: the early deaths of several family members including his only son; the Great Depression; WWII; and then US occupation.

The family background of Haier's Zhang Ruimin is equally humble. He was born to factory worker parents during the closing months of China's civil war, shortly before the establishment of the People's Republic. His formative years were punctuated by the tumults of the country's ideological campaigns like the Great Leap Forward and the Cultural Revolution.

Some of the future leaders' childhood deprivation stemmed from being raised in single parent or otherwise incomplete families. Stan Shih lost his father at the age of four. For Ratan Tata the dominant female figure of his childhood was his grandmother, who raised him after his parents split up. Interestingly, literature on leadership has documented many instances of successful leaders having supportive mothers and absent fathers.[10]

The Spartan conditions that marked these individuals' formative years are perhaps most discernible in their limited schooling. Nonetheless, where opportunities for formal learning were severely limited, they sought out other, informal sources of knowledge. When denied access to higher education, for instance, Chung Ju-yung learned at his grandfather's Confucian school and later on by reading business documents.

It is conceivable that this lack of formal education opportunities was one of the influencing factors that later motivated these leaders to seek out avenues leading to lifelong learning. Thus Zhang Ruimin completed an MBA program at a local university while working full time as general manager. He remains a voracious reader of new books on management and innovation. Masamoto Yashiro was in his seventies when he learned Mandarin while working with corporations in China. For Ratan Tata, a lifelong dedication to learning was one of the lynchpins of his successful leadership at Tata Sons.

In many of these stories of resilience developed in the face of dramatic hardship, it seems that this led to the development of an ability to make sacrifices in the short term in the interest of long-term benefit.

Early Childhood Exposure to Business

Regardless of whether their childhood was constrained by material shortage or not, early exposure to industrial techniques and processes, albeit on a modest scale, seems instrumental to many of our central characters' future professional pursuits.

For example, Eiji Toyoda was raised in his father's textile mill, which gave him exposure to machines and business. For the rest of his life, he retained a unique ability to spot and minimize waste. In his book, *Inside the Mind of Toyota*, he says: "Problems are rolling all around in front of your eyes. Whether you pick them up and treat them as problems is a matter of habit. If you have the habit, then you can do whatever you have a mind to."[11] He expressed a similar passion for making things better in an interview for the 1986 book, *Kaizen*: "Our workers provide 1.5 million suggestions a year, and 95 percent of them are put to practical use. There is an almost tangible concern for improvement in the air at Toyota."[12] Meanwhile, the young Chung Ju-yung, later of Hyundai, was drawn to the construction industry, as he felt that this was an environment where he could start from scratch.[13]

Interestingly, throughout their lives and careers, several of these leaders not only acknowledged that the hardship they experienced was a character-building influence and a source of great discipline, but also consciously sought to repeat and replicate many of its habits and rituals.

Chung Ju-yung is a case in point. Despite his personal wealth of several billion dollars, he lived in a simple home, never took up expensive hobbies, and encouraged staff at Hyundai to put aside 30–40 percent of their pay checks into savings accounts.[14] A disciplinarian, he would wake at 3 a.m. every day and walk three miles to work. This was the same routine he had developed as a youngster in his poverty-stricken village where physical survival itself was difficult. Equally strict with others as he was with himself, he demanded 15-hour workdays from his executives.

Chung Ju-yung was far from alone in his self-imposed simplicity of life. Those who knew Konosuke Matsushita described him without exception as unassuming in his appearance, voice, and demeanor.

In a similar vein, having brought his company to dizzying heights of success, Eiji Toyoda continued to avoid the limelight as well as opportunities to assert the company's role through political lobbying. He often turned down interview requests and generally tried to diminish the perception of Toyota's dominant position, not only on the international stage but also domestically.[15]

Under Toyoda's leadership, Toyota came to describe itself, and the automotive industry, as "a green tomato – incomplete and growing."[16] Likewise, Ratan Tata has been reported to be just as disdainful of pretense and status symbols, choosing to travel alone even on long business trips.

Memory of Childhood Deprivation as a Source of Strength

Reading about their childhood experiences, one develops a strong sense that even if granted a wish, these leaders would not have traded the "school of hard knocks" for anything.

Zhang Ruimin described the extent to which the Cultural Revolution affected him, as a high school student when it began, teaching him to persist in the face of difficulties. Rather than becoming arrogant or excessively optimistic, it helped him to reflect deeply on his role in the world, and to develop a more tolerant approach to failure. In fact, it instilled in him a deep sense of resilience. In Zhang's own words, "We learned that everything can turn for the better and all kinds of challenges can be overcome. There is no crisis that cannot be resolved."[17]

Likewise, Chung Ju-yung's abortive escapes from his native village taught him to view setbacks only as signals that extra effort was needed the next time. Even the string of personal tragedies that Konosuke Matsushita experienced ultimately taught him to face difficulty head on.

The often tough childhood experiences of our profiled steward leaders proved to be profoundly inspiring. At the same time, stepping out of their own culture and traveling overseas to further their education played an equally defining role in shaping their emerging stewardship profile.

At the age of 15, in the middle of the initial outburst of China's modernizing May Fourth Movement of 1919, Deng Xiaoping joined a group of Chinese students – among them, several of his future fellow revolutionaries – to travel to France and enroll in local schools.

Jaime Zóbel de Alaya attended British boarding schools and tertiary institutions in the United States. Shinsei Bank's Masamoto Yashiro also received early post-war exposure to the United States. With a grant received from the Committee for a Free Asia (now the Asia Foundation), he attended the 1952 National Student Conference held at Indiana University in Bloomington.

The personality of Mitsubishi's Minoru Makihara was similarly shaped by a childhood spent overseas. A child of a Mitsubishi manager who had been posted on an overseas assignment, Makihara was born in England and received a Western education including a degree from Harvard. In this respect, he was not alone: Ratan Tata graduated from Cornell University and Harvard Business School.

A fellow Harvard Business School graduate, Victor Fung, received his undergraduate degree from MIT. Singapore statesman Lee Kuan Yew graduated with a law degree from Cambridge – where he was known among friends and colleagues as Harry Lee – and returned to Singapore in 1949. His parents and grandparents were English-educated. Lee and his wife spoke English as their mother tongue and Malay as the colony's *lingua franca*. He learned Chinese in his early thirties. He never denied the difficulty involved in mastering the language as a mature student, and has talked openly about the struggles and insights from his learning experience.

There are, of course, exceptions to the rule. Notably, Stan Shih. At a time when many of his peers chose to pursue university degrees in North America, he remained in Taiwan where the focus of his studies was on mathematics and R&D.[18] Shih enjoyed his time at a relaunched local university because he felt it gave him the opportunity to "create something out of nothing." Interestingly, too, he defines his experiences during this time as instrumental in preparing him for the future challenges of running Acer.[19]

Agility through a Multicultural Mind-Set

Although a result of similar learning experiences and international exposure rather than a personality trait, a significant number of the steward leaders in our group were effectively bicultural as well as bilingual. His US venture capital partners have described Shinsei Bank's Masamoto Yashiro as "completely cross-cultural," equally at ease with the nuances of Japanese and American business.[20] By his own admission, when engineering Shinsei's turnaround and relaunch, Yashiro "didn't do things the Japanese way."[21] He came to be recognized as an internationally minded person; a global citizen; someone who could quickly identify the linkages between industries and national economies.

In a similar twist of fate, UK-born Minoru Makihara was another leader who turned ambiguity into strength. He arrived at Harvard in the post-war years, during a period of lingering animosity but also growing curiosity towards Japan. Thanks to his language skills and cosmopolitan outlook, he became known for the rest of his career as "a guy the Americans like."[22] At the same time, he would sometimes describe himself as "quintessentially Japanese."

In addition to his role as a statesman, Lee Kuan Yew established a reputation as a prolific writer and engaging storyteller with a passion for sharing his analysis, vision, and predictions for international economics and politics. Among other things, he became a sought-after authority on the geopolitics involving the United States and China. Meanwhile, the Fung brothers of Li & Fung, although based in Asia, are US nationals and consider themselves Chinese-American.

Beyond bilingual and bicultural considerations, it seems a standard feature of many of the compelling stories of steward leadership in Asia that, at one point or another, many attempted to put forward a synthesis between their native world view and the acquired, largely Western theory of management and organizational behavior. In the process, they may have rejected elements of one culture or another. Either way, the act of taking stock of their knowledge and aiming to reinterpret it in a creative way, in many cases years ahead of theory or relevant comparative studies, appears to be one of the genuine hallmarks of Asia's steward leaders. It also speaks volumes about their intellectual curiosity, prowess, and discipline. The sense of cultural flexibility they have cultivated has sensitized them to different mindsets, thus sharpening their ability to understand and to adapt to different contexts quickly.

Synthesizing Western and Asian Management

In a large measure, Minoru Makihara's success was the result of his ability to synthesize the best aspects of Western management with Japanese tradition. For example, he was passionate about forging a new Japanese model of corporate responsibility, drawing on Western systems of corporate governance.[23] He viewed the global economy as essentially built on relationships; advocated mutual foreign investment among countries; and regarded difficult economic times as opportunities for new ideas, synergies, and business relationships.

Perhaps more than his company's success in capturing a sizable chunk of global market share in its product segments, Zhang Ruimin is also known for combining Western management precepts with uniquely Chinese ideas about running an organization. Likewise,

Ratan Tata's overseas training as an architect instilled in him a deep preference for the rational, the transparent, and the systematic.

In some instances, the knowledge that there is more than one way to approach a situation served to nurture a contrarian streak in steward leaders' characters. Masamoto Yashiro observed: "[Japanese] people don't like dealing with people like me. They think I am American"[24] and "I never wanted to be part of corporate Japan."[25]

An agent of change in a conservative Japanese industry, Yashiro was committed to business transparency. He introduced bottom-line indicators, to be measured on a monthly basis against each of the bank's business segments and products, and pushed to have this information shared with employees at all levels through a completely overhauled IT system.[26]

A self-declared social liberal, he has put his provocative streak to good use by advocating social causes such as enhancing women's roles and responsibilities in Japanese corporate life; liberalizing Japan's immigration policy; and promoting the use of English as a tool of global communication. He has also been vocal about environmental protection and good corporate governance.

Steward Leaders Connect through Compassion

How did the steward leaders we have discussed approach their followers in order to arrive at a shared sense of "we"? What attitudes, character traits, and prior experiences did they draw on when engaging with large groups of followers?

In Stan Shih's words, "you can create more problems being harsh, being ... demanding or without any feeling at all." He believes in "very logical thinking with a little bit of the warm heart."[27] The "warm heart" reflects an understanding of fellow humans, and of oneself, as thriving on social, emotional, and community attention and support.

Compassion is a central characteristic of steward leaders, who display empathy in their interactions with others.

Steward leaders view compassion and empathy not as something that is given from one to another out of pity but rather as a bridge to understanding the connection humans have with one another. Nelson Mandela put it eloquently: "Our human compassion binds us the one to the other – not in pity or patronizingly, but as human beings who have learnt how to turn our common suffering into hope for the future."[28]

Culturally, acknowledging the social and emotional factors behind producing a sense of "we" may have been easier for leaders in Asia than in Western societies. Unlike the West, the Asian tradition never had the tendency, or felt the need, to compartmentalize life's experiences into public vs. private, religious vs. secular, personal vs. work-related.

American philosopher Ken Wilber sums up the general non-Western view of this obsessive yet typically unconscious compartmentalization: "We create a persistent alienation from ourselves, from others and from the world by fracturing our present experience into different parts separated by boundaries. We artificially split our awareness into compartments such as subject vs. object, life vs. death, mind vs. body, inside vs. outside, reason vs. instinct ..."[29]

Asia's steward leaders appear to have been equipped with the appropriate tools to nurture a shared sense of achievement, meaning, and purpose in their organizations; to draw out ideas, opinions, problems, and solutions; and to use conversations and dialogue to transmit their personal as well as organizational values.[30]

According to Zhang Ruimin, who is often branded the Philosopher CEO: "Coming of age in the Cultural Revolution, I of course missed the opportunity to attend university and was thrown abruptly to the bottom of working society. There is no question in my mind that those years exerted a significant influence on how I now go about leading others. When I dine with Haier workers, as I do nearly every day, or when I drop in unannounced at a workplace, I am always looking to renew my understanding of their perspective."[31]

Many of the steward leaders who emerged from the destruction of WWII and its aftermath not only led by example but also literally embodied and breathed their organizations' core values. They created and passed down powerful symbols that have been a shared source of meaning for their companies' employees ever since, such as a country's first shipping container terminal; a first locally manufactured calculator; or a globally competitive passenger car. In other words, they knew that the "how" of arriving was just as important as the destination or the goal itself.[32]

Understanding the Human Capacity to Grow and Learn

Even more importantly, steward leaders do not consider the natural state of things to be one of stability. They understand well that humans seek to learn and grow, not keep things and themselves the same.[33] The story, by now immortalized in many books and journal articles, of Zhang Ruimin's exhorting his workers to smash faulty products to smithereens, makes for a colorful anecdote when teaching executives about China's economic transformation.

In reality, it was about so much more than that. The group act of applying brutal physical force to a shared problem was in its own way a powerful ritual, reinforcing a nascent organizational culture of strict quality standards. It sent a strong signal that the old, lackadaisical ways of unclear task and quality ownership would no longer be tolerated. If the company was to survive, the old mind-set had to be annihilated along with the defective merchandise.

This deep-seated confidence in the ability and the continuous desire – in fact, the basic human need – of one's followers to learn and improve, and to rise to challenges is a defining aspect of steward leaders. In many cases, it is also what informed and shaped their attitude to risk.

In taking over the reins of Singapore's government on August 9, 1965, Prime Minister Lee Kuan Yew publicly shared in his countrymen's anxiety and anguish over the prospects facing a small nation that had national independence thrust on her but was otherwise left to her own devices.

At the same time, he had the gift of reading clearly the new country's collective aspirations, which included: establishing itself as a permanent home to many members of Southeast Asia's Straits Chinese community as well as other races, whose status in history had up to that point been largely one of sojourners; retaining the modern, business-friendly frameworks and institutions of its recent past as a Crown territory, including a secular government and the English language; and building on the legacy of the country's immigrant forefathers to uphold and strengthen its place as an international hub of trade, commerce, and transport in a freshly decolonized world.

"Take small steps and remain grounded"

China's former Paramount Leader Deng Xiaoping expressed a similar sentiment and a similar outlook on risk when he said "We are crossing the river by feeling each stone." A shrewd psychologist, Deng tapped into the collective consciousness of the Chinese people, exhausted and demoralized after years of being exposed to constant ideological war and propaganda, and craving some basic, universal security markers such as private ownership, personal space, individual lifestyle, and opinion. His main initial contribution was in the form of calming down the previously shrill and fanatical state rhetoric as well as the international political landscape involving China.

The metaphor about stepping stones cutting a path across a river neatly captured the fundamental nature of the country's ambitious program of reform and liberalization that was unfolding under Deng's leadership. Though possessing a long-term vision, but attempting a far-reaching project that had never been undertaken before, and with the long-term well-being of a billion people at stake, even the top leader could only assess situations one at a time, in a grounded and incremental way, and expect unfathomable and unintended developments along the way. The saying contained distinct echoes of the classical Chinese dictum: "When you know, say that you know it; when you do not know, admit that you do not know it. That is knowledge."[34]

Some of Deng Xiaoping's policies and communication strategies continue to provide good examples of co-opting stakeholder (in this case, citizen) values; and of engaging stakeholders by talking about values and explaining how they underpin specific decision-making processes. This combination of skills enabled Deng to preside over what was possibly the only time in history when large-scale economic liberalization was successfully introduced within the political environment of an autocratic state, without derailing either segment. He succeeded in quietly dismantling the personality cult of Mao Zedong while acknowledging Mao's legacy as "70 percent positive." He also set the precedent of removing his political adversaries through retirement rather than persecution, and initiated tentative models for political succession so that the country's leaders would no longer remain in power for life. He understood that negotiating a solution to Hong Kong's return to Chinese rule would restore much pride to the people of China and bolster his own nationalist and leadership credentials.

Today, Deng Xiaoping has captured the West's postmodern imagination to such an extent that some have described him as "a leader who saw a future, went against the tide, and used the levers of influence he had to gamble on a complete retro-fitting and relaunch of China."[35]

Universally, the steward leaders featured in our vignettes are "truly human enough" to use their power for positive social influence.[36] It is hardly surprising that independently of each other, several of them have spoken for years about their desire ultimately to cast aside the majority of structures, systems, and processes. They will settle, however, for the next best thing, which is to knock these structures off their pedestal at the center of the organization and shift them to a place where they always belonged – one that supports the company's vision and mission, as well as the autonomous employee groups of the type we have seen at Haier.

Haier's Zhang Ruimin believed in the importance of employees finding a deep sense of connection to the company, as a way to fulfill individual values while creating value for the company. For him, beyond supervision or growth, the ultimate protection against company failure was the ability to infuse employees with a sense of their own value through the company's value: "Size is no protection against failure if you are not able to fill each employee with vitality." His vision was to create a company where employees used Haier as a global platform to create their own value, believing this would be a major source of competitive advantage. Central to his aim was to instill employees with a sense of autonomy, to eventually become "a populace unaware of the presence of their ruler."[37]

PART

III

STEWARDSHIP IN ACTION

CHAPTER
6

Stewardship Actions

Stewardship in an organization is built on strong values and personalities. But ultimately, the real test of stewardship is not only in being or believing but also in doing. A popular saying is that "managers and leaders who fail generally do so not because of things they don't know, but because of things they know perfectly well that they just aren't doing."[1] In the words of Hyundai's founder Chung Ju-yung: "In the real world of business, success can only be achieved through action. Businesses cannot grow merely by sitting around and thinking about what has to be done. Action must come first."[2]

Action is the vehicle that materializes steward leaders' deep-seated beliefs. It is action that propagates ideas and transmits values and principles to employees, partners, and local communities. Action captures and disseminates knowledge inside and outside the organization, and channels investment to learning and development programs. Action gives people a personalized image of the company so that they can respond with loyalty and commitment.

Steward leaders understand that living and breathing a particular set of values can serve as an inspiration to others, but truly sharing and transmitting values to their workforce requires action. More importantly, they recognize that whatever rules, initiatives, or proclamations management has come up with, these only represent one side of the story, the "top down" traffic of ideas and information. Much of this information is objective and analytical, drawing on facts and research, but it is also impersonal.

Therefore the rest (or the missing part) of the story has been likened to a huge underground river. This is the "real world" of employees' informal communications, conversations, and other exchanges, a virtual public arena where the company's staff make sense of things and form an understanding of what the leadership's decisions really mean to them, their families, and the company. In shaping this understanding, people engage not only their rational faculties that respond to cool analysis but also their aspirations, hopes, and fears. This is a key ingredient of every organization's health. The fact that it is so often overlooked and ignored by management, which focuses on the rational, written, fact- and outcome-based version of events, explains why the majority of company-wide change management programs fail to achieve all of their original objectives.

One cynic observed that "the modern workplace is a collection of new technologies, new business strategies, and new leadership methodologies ... and the same staggering number of disengaged employees."[3]

Helping Employees Find Meaning through Narratives

One type of leadership action that has seen resurgence in recent years has to do with fashioning powerful narratives. To give their best to their work, people must be able to look to work as a source of meaning. Narratives are a method for weaving seemingly random, isolated scraps of information, knowledge, and experience into a meaningful thread. Since the dawn of history, humans have arranged their observations of life's events into tales of heroes who do battle with enemies, overcome obstacles, and finally achieve their goals. Well-structured stories are increasingly acknowledged as fundamental to the human search for meaning.[4]

In structuring a compelling narrative, it helps to revisit and find a good balance among Aristotle's four elements of good rhetoric: *ethos* (the speaker's character and credibility); *pathos* (appealing to the reader's or listener's sympathy and power of imagination); *logos* (clarity and logical consistency of the message); and *agora* (reflecting the setting, timing, culture, and venue).

Strong narratives can often take the form of parables; they can invoke a sense of community as well as create an effect that is emotionally moving. Throughout, they serve to nurture an individual's whole person, including "spirit and soul" and the need to find deep personal meaning, purpose, and a sense of community as a way to counter the frequently atomizing, isolating, and impersonal nature of work in modern-day organizations.

Vehicles for Building Trust

In Asian organizations, using stories as a way for a leader to tell others "who he/she is" in terms of background, values, family status, and other characteristics gives the leader particularly strong leverage in terms of goodwill and trust to draw on in the future. As we have noted, Asian societies have little regard for dividing and isolating parts of one's experience into work vs. private life, business vs. family and so on.

Modern-day strategists of human resources management in markets like China have likewise pointed out that in this part of the world, a team of employees has to feel comfortable socially before it can start functioning well professionally. In a region that has led the world in the adoption of information technology and smart communication devices, it is also worth considering social media as an increasingly compelling platform for telling the world about who the leader is and what a company stands for.

Bridging the Gap between Management and Employee Narratives

The truth is that every employee constructs their own reality. This reality is influenced by shared, objective, material factors just as much as it is by the employee's own assumptions, perceptions, attitudes, and interpretations. Material rewards and incentives can certainly influence and improve a person's performance up to a point, typically in the measureable, transactional aspects of day-to-day work. But to stir and stimulate what is truly important (yet invisible) to the employee, the organization's leadership must exert a motivating force. It needs to make any large-scale, dramatic change appear familiar and desirable.

Employees cannot be coerced to feel highly motivated and fully engaged. Leaders must appeal to the individual's values, outlining how they relate to the company's values, and guide them toward bridging and internalizing the two. Bridging official, top-down systems to informal, bottom-up narratives is an essential task for a steward leader.

In *The Leader's Guide to Storytelling*, Steve Denning, a former World Bank executive, comments: "Analysis might excite the mind, but it hardly offers a route to the heart. And that's where we must go if we are to motivate people not only to take action but to do so with energy and enthusiasm. At a time when corporate survival often requires disruptive change, leadership involves inspiring people to act in unfamiliar, and often unwelcome, ways. Mind-numbing cascades of numbers or daze-inducing PowerPoint slides won't achieve this goal. Even logical arguments for making the needed changes usually won't do the trick."[5]

Stories could help leaders define their personality, boosting confidence in their integrity and providing some idea of how they might act in a given situation.[6] But ultimately, what counts is aligning the words with actions.

Documenting, Sharing, and Disseminating Knowledge

Another crucial aspect of internally focused steward leadership action, and one that is very relevant today, has to do with documenting, sharing, and disseminating knowledge. Many of Asia's leading companies originated as small, family-owned businesses. As they expanded, political uncertainties might have led the majority of them to diversify across a number of unrelated industries as a way of protecting their assets. In the process, it was tantalizingly easy to displace a great deal of the company founder's original, specialist knowledge and expertise. Often, this kind of knowledge is described as "tacit." Given that the founder was likely to have started the company as a one-person operation, the likelihood of his having had the time or the means to write down what was in his head is very slim. As a result, it may require an entire generation of owners to piece this knowledge back together, write it down, organize it, and regularly run it through the entire organization.

Kuan Mun Leong, managing director of Malaysian glove-maker Hartalega, explained how his father had, in the past, kept firm control over the company, with a few select trusted advisers. These advisers (who had worked for him for over 20 years) had internalized his knowledge and way of thinking, and served as the company's "gatekeepers." This meant that they would only intervene on the factory floor when there was disruption, quickly retreating to their offices after issuing instructions. While this had worked well when the company was small, increasing scale (from 10 to 55 production lines since the IPO) made this impossible, with increasing numbers of employees (including engineers and executives). Kuan Mun Leong commented on the implications of this change: "That's why we need a strategy for knowledge transfer – what used to be a pyramid must now give way to an expansive structure."[7]

Even more complex is the fact that to grow, learning has to take place from across a spectrum of sources. This was one of the key priorities for Japan's Shinsei Bank after Masamoto Yashiro took over as CEO. He brought together know-how from all over the world, and pushed through policies aimed at attracting talent and expertise regardless of nationality. His view was that: "You have to have different nationalities. ... I never ask what school they went to; whether they are a man or a woman; I only ask what they can do."[8]

While it is a challenge, it remains important to the stewardship of an organization to find an effective way not only to acquire knowledge widely but also to document and share accumulated experiences.

Sharing and Adopting Best Practices

Robust learning architectures typically give rise to another phenomenon that goes hand in hand with stewardship – best practices. The notion of leading the way, as well as studying and replicating industry best practice from a variety of worldwide sources, speaks to the very heart of steward leadership.

By definition, sharing best practices transcends not only the boundaries of one's company but also those of the present time, fueling innovation and growth across entire industry segments and related ecosystems. As early as the 1960s, Konosuke Matsushita hosted visits to his company's operations in Japan by foreign leaders including US Attorney General Robert Kennedy, Indian Prime Minister Indira Gandhi, and Yugoslavian President Josip Broz Tito.

Similarly, Eiji Toyoda built on the experience gained in Toyota's US joint venture to test the viability of the company's production philosophies when applied to different cultures. Despite the Cold War, the long-standing tensions in US–Japan trade, and the visceral instinct of many businesses that originated as family-owned structures to "keep one's cards close to the chest," Eiji Toyoda's philosophy of learning was open and reciprocal. He first inspected Ford's factory in the United States in the early 1950s and, following the launch of

Toyota's successful passenger car models, scores of teams from around the world toured Toyota's Japanese factories to gain first-hand exposure to new management principles such as just-in-time assembly and lean supply chain management.

The act of sharing best practices and thought leadership insights is not limited to trade and industry. Widely respected for his unique and often prescient perspectives on international relations and other developments, Singapore's Lee Kuan Yew was a mentor to every Chinese leader from Deng Xiaoping to Xi Jinping, and a counselor to every US president from Richard Nixon to Barack Obama.[9] He was sought out for his ideas on trends and developments that shape today's global agenda, particularly the evolving nature of business competitiveness, the rise of Asian economies, and China's ongoing transformation into a 21st-century superpower.

Meanwhile, Shinsei's Masamoto Yashiro has been equally passionate about sharing some of Japan's recent hard-earned development lessons in post-bubble economic growth with other countries in Asia and Europe that are striving to forestall stagnation and deflation scenarios in their own national economies. This is also what motivated Yashiro to accept an outside director position on the board of the China Construction Bank. As he commented: "Some of the post-bubble problems of the Japanese banks perhaps looked similar to those of the large state-owned banks."[10] His countryman, Mitsubishi's Minoru Makihara, also worked to apply his experience to developing societies, serving on the International Investment Committee of President Thabo Mbeki of South Africa and on the Millennium Board established by the President of Colombia.

Building Brands

Externally, steward leaders seek to uphold their personal values and their organization's values by investing in and building strong brands. A brand is "a promise" between the company and its stakeholders. It may have been part instinct, part unconscious thinking, but this is clearly what drove business leaders like Stan Shih to become discontented with the OEM model, despite its popularity across Asia's manufacturing hubs at the time. Considering Asian companies' history of pragmatism and established focus on tangibles, it took time for them to embrace concepts like brand equity. Indeed, the creation of world-renowned brands during the postwar era can be ranked among the principal acts of stewardship in Asia.

The shift toward according branding the place it deserves in the corporate world is still in progress. According to Martin Roll (author of *Asian Brand Strategy*) it necessitates a change in mindsets: "From a tactical view to a long-term, strategic perspective, from fragmented marketing activities to totally aligned branding activities, from a vision of branding as the sole responsibility of marketing managers to branding as the most essential function of the firm led by the boardroom."[11]

Supporting the strategy of building strong brand names are business leaders' actions aimed at making their beliefs and ideas accessible and available through books, interviews, and magazine articles. In addition to the brand-building component, contributing content to publications has allowed leaders to influence their industry and introduce new paradigms of thought. Some of the steward leaders' seminal books have been instrumental not only in promoting their companies' growth but also in pushing boundaries and in some cases changing the rules of the game for entire industries, communities, and countries.

For instance, in addition to his activities as a prolific author and educator, Konosuke Matsushita launched PHP Intersect magazine as an attempt to universalize his ideas. Book titles like *The Toyota Way* have become required reading for global managers. And Lee Kuan Yew's *The Singapore Story* captured the imagination of statesmen and policymakers worldwide.

Supporting a Global Network of Learning

We discussed steward leaders' propensity for lifelong learning, which was undiminished even in the face of great hardship. Contemporary steward leaders have made, and continue to make, substantial investments in learning institutions, networks, and other learning platforms. Because many of the leaders received overseas education, and because their ambition is to effect positive change not only in their home communities and countries but also around the world, the combined network of these institutions today spans the globe.

For example, Jaime Zóbel de Ayala has been an active alumnus of Harvard College and Harvard Business School. He worked with not only his *alma mater* in the United States but also with leading universities and business schools in Southeast Asia, holding director and trustee positions with Singapore Management University (SMU) and the Asian Institute of Management (Philippines).

For his part, Ratan Tata has been a member of the Harvard Business School India Advisory Board; trustee of several top-ranked US universities; member of the Board of Governors of the East-West Center; president of the Court of the Indian Institute of Science and chairman of the Council of Management of the Tata Institute of Fundamental Research; as well as member of the jury of the prestigious Pritzker Prize for architectural design. Ratan Tata's great-grandfather, Jamsetji Tata, played an instrumental role in setting up the Indian Institute of Science, the Tata Institute of Fundamental Research, and the Tata Institute of Social Sciences.

Established in 1979 by Panasonic's founder, by then 84-year-old Konosuke Matsushita, the Matsushita Institute of Government and Management seeks to promote and develop 21st-century leadership. Building on the values of its founder, the school has embraced an innovative approach to education and leadership in order to foster profound change in Japanese society and its relationship with the rest of the world. It has come to be acknowledged and emulated as "a place where the leaders of the future could create clear national and international policies, as well as the programs for their realization, to bring lasting benefit to the citizens of Japan and the world."[12] In 2011, Yoshihiko Noda became the school's first graduate to be appointed Japan's Prime Minister.

Elsewhere, Mitsubishi's Minoru Makihara has supported scholarship on Asia. He became director general of the Toyo Bunko, one of the world's leading libraries dedicated to Asian studies, and made a significant investment in Mitsubishi Corporation Japanese Galleries at the British Museum. Meanwhile, in 2004, the National University of Singapore (NUS) set up the Lee Kuan Yew School of Public Policy, a graduate school with a mission to "educate and inspire current and future generations of leaders to raise the standards of governance in Asia, improve the lives of its people and contribute to the transformation of the region."[13]

Some steward leaders have striven to further their causes by combining their real-life business experience with academic rigor. Among them, Victor Fung of Li & Fung, the third-generation owner of a controlling stake in a family business that was founded in 1906, has been particularly passionate about education and nurturing the next generation of leaders. While chairman of the Council of the University of Hong Kong, he worked to reform the school's governance structure and to raise the school's profile and reputation globally. He also held a number of other positions including being a member of the Economic Development Commission of the Hong Kong Government and chairman (2008–2010) of the Paris-based International Chamber of Commerce. Not surprisingly, his expertise has been sought after by China's public sector agencies and the country's top-ranked universities including Peking University, Tsinghua University, and Renmin University.

Philanthropy: The Business of Doing Good

Philanthropic initiatives by well-stewarded companies serve to support long-standing needs of communities. These initiatives reflect the focus on social good as one of the lynchpins of stewardship. More broadly, they represent steward leaders' deeply-held, essential view of business as a force for good. In the past few years, global entrepreneurs like Richard Branson have promoted a range of business models aimed at "doing good," such as purpose-driven businesses, social enterprises, value-based businesses, and catalytic organizations. According to Branson: "Businesses can be a force for good and shouldn't think of themselves as just worrying about the bottom line profit."[14]

In pursuing these new initiatives and business models, business leaders are standing on the shoulders of giants. For instance, the Ayala Foundation has a history of more than 50 years, having started life as the Filipinas Foundation in 1961. It cites "cultural and civic patronage as one of the most enduring characteristics of the Ayala heritage." The foundation describes itself as a catalyst for inclusion to bridge community and business aspirations, and lists a "deep love of [our] country" at the top of its list of values.[15]

In Korea, Hyundai founder Chung Ju-yung set up his Asan Social Welfare Foundation in 1977 with the aim of providing basic social welfare for those most in need by building hospitals in remote areas and offering scholarships to disadvantaged students. In addition to medical support and scholarship funds, the foundation, modeled on the Ford and Rockefeller charitable trusts in the United States, also provided social welfare and R&D assistance. Chung Ju-yung served as the foundation's chairman until his death in 2001. Working under the motto "there are no failures, only trials," the foundation has since given rise to offshoots such as the Asan Medical Center, Asan Entrepreneurship Forum, Asan Academy, and other organizations.

Chung also served five terms as president of the Federation of Korean Industries (1977–1987).

Similarly, the Tata founders bequeathed most of their personal wealth to a number of trusts they created for the greater good of India and its people. Today, the Tata Trusts control 66 percent of the shares of Tata Sons, the holding Tata company. Ratan Tata continues to serve as chairman of the Tata Trusts, supporting a wide range of education institutions as well as social and community causes.

On a practical level, some steward leaders have not only extended their help to the philanthropic and voluntary sectors, but have also shared their business acumen and expertise. Thus Masamoto Yashiro accepted a director position at New York Philharmonic; Toyota, as part of its community service programs, trained workers at the Food Bank for New York City in ways to optimize work flow and quality; and Bill Gates introduced rigorous evaluation techniques into the philanthropic activities of the Gates Foundation.

Keepers of the Culture

Ultimately, all of these types of leadership action place steward leaders in the position of "keepers of the culture," tasked with building an organizational memory that supports and reinforces the valued rules and behaviors.[16] In this position, a leader like Eiji Toyoda would still come into his office in his nineties in order to exercise his role as honorary chairman and honorary advisor. At this time, he devoted many of his company visits to discussions with his younger successors. Even when ill and hospitalized, he continued sending emails to Toyota managers, offering advice and encouragement.[17] He also chaired the company's commemorative museum.

Other notable steward leaders who had retired came out of retirement when circumstances and their organization's well-being dictated it. For example, Masamoto Yashiro agreed to return to Shinsei as part-time chairman in 2008 to help deal with the crisis and to augment the new president's leadership. Despite the fact that he had already retired prior to joining Shinsei for the first time, in his own words, he had "never worked harder."[18]

More recently, in November 2013, Stan Shih temporarily, and over-riding his spouse's objections, returned to Acer as interim president and chairman, after 10 years in retirement, to assist the company's restructuring process.

Outside the scope of their organizations, steward leaders actively shape the discourse, narratives, and priorities of national as well as global business and politics by sharing their views with international forums. For instance, Jaime Zóbel de Ayala has represented the Philippines in regional and global business structures such as the World Economic Forum and APEC Business Advisory Council. At the end of his term as president and CEO in 1998, Minoru Makihara became Mitsubishi Corporation's chairman for six years, a position that enabled him to be a strong voice in government and in international business affairs alongside his other roles such as chairman of the Japan-US Business Council. In India, Ratan Tata has been a member of the Prime Minister's Council on Trade and Industry and the National Manufacturing Competitiveness Council.

Li & Fung's Fung brothers have long been considered to be veritable global citizens, not just because of their frequent travels and diverse domiciles but also because of their dedication to civic causes worldwide. Victor Fung was co-chair of former Swiss-based The Evian Group@IMD, which aimed to create a "bridge between north and south" and brought together corporate, government, and opinion leaders. Founded in 1995, The Evian Group@IMD bills itself as committed to "fostering an open, inclusive, equitable and sustainable global market economy supported by a rules-based multilateral framework."

An active public speaker who likes to share his ideas locally as well as internationally, Victor Fung has been a member of the Informal Business Advisory Body to the World Trade Organization, and has participated in the Hong Kong chapter of the Clinton Global Initiative and the Clinton Global Citizen Awards. Dedicated to producing and promoting innovative research and thinking on Chinese and Asian business, he set up the Li & Fung Research Centre as a knowledge resource focused on China's economy. He is also founding chairman, through the philanthropic Victor and William Fung Foundation, of the Fung Global Institute, an independent, non-profit think tank based in Hong Kong that generates and disseminates innovative thinking and research on global issues from Asian perspectives.

Fostering Global Harmony

Steward leaders also direct their actions towards promoting harmony, empathy, and understanding between cultures, faiths, and nations.

Thus Chung Ju-yung lobbied on his country's behalf to win the right to host the 1988 summer Olympics, and was subsequently awarded an IOC medallion for his contribution to international sports as a vehicle of understanding. He was committed to normalizing relations between the two Koreas, despite the absence of legitimate avenues for extending economic assistance to the people of North Korea.

Eiji Toyoda also sought harmony and compromise in international business relations. He tried to establish partnerships with US automakers such as Ford well before WWII. In the 1980s, his response to the escalating trade tensions between Japan and the United States was to establish a joint venture with GM in a defunct plant in Fremont, California.

Another champion of cultural exchange between Japan and the West, Minoru Makihara, chaired CULCON, the US-Japan Conference on Cultural and Educational Interchange, established by John F. Kennedy and the then Prime Minister Hayato Ikeda to strengthen the bilateral relationship through enhanced exchanges.

Konosuke Matsushita devoted his retirement (he retired in 1961, at the age of 65) to creating Japan's version of the Nobel Prize[19] and to establishing the PHP Institute ("Peace and Happiness through Prosperity") as well as activities in book publishing and events management. His ambition was to understand human nature and its implications for management, public policy, and everyday life. The PHP Institute was set up in 1946 with a remit to address "fundamental questions concerning the human condition."[20] It started publishing its own magazine the following year. Thinking deeply about the imperatives of individual and social life through the institute's activities as well as related writings – his *Thoughts on Man* came out in 1974 – Matsushita predicted very early on that the 21st century would be a time of prosperity for Asia.[21]

Becoming a Steward Leader – What It Takes

There is no template for steward leadership. The steward leaders described throughout this book are vastly different in terms of personality characteristics and styles. But, crucially, they share three key characteristics.

First, they are transformational leaders who inspire their followers to excel and achieve superior performance through their charisma, inspiration, intellectual stimulation, and individualized consideration. We call this leading with impact.

Second, through a combination of prudence and care, steward leaders safeguard the future and ensure that the organization and its stakeholders thrive over the long term. They exercise their judgment and discipline to sacrifice short-term profits for long-term gain. This enables the organization to regenerate over time.

Finally, by exercising transparency, accountability, and responsibility, steward leaders demonstrate a deep understanding of the organization's broader social impact to bring about positive social change in spheres beyond the organization. This is the third trait common to steward leaders.

Steward leaders are essential to instigating and sustaining stewardship over time. They ensure that their organizations foster positive relationships with stakeholders both internally and externally, building the necessary continuity and maintaining organizational momentum.

This chapter aims to help aspiring steward leaders understand and reflect on their strengths and weaknesses across the dimensions of stewardship. To identify developmental gaps, we introduce a questionnaire to help you better understand potential blind spots, to support you on your journey to become a steward leader and secure your legacy.

The Idea of Leadership

Before looking at stewardship at the individual level, it is helpful to quickly review leadership theory. The early days of leadership focused on the traits of successful leaders, their behaviors and/or styles. Then we had theories of situational and functional leadership, which advocated adapting leadership to the task, individual, group, or unit at hand. While these are useful concepts, there are always successful leaders who seem to be the anomaly, defying classification in these areas, or where these conditions are not applicable.

Many theories of leadership focus on what is effective in terms of leadership behavior, as well as the structures that leaders put in place at the organizational level. We have listed some of the main leadership theories in Table 7.1. This list includes the characteristics of Transactional,[1] Transformational,[2] Servant,[3] Authentic,[4] Adaptive,[5] Shared Leadership,[6] and Transcendent Leadership[7] behaviors. This list is not intended to be exhaustive; rather its purpose is to review some of the characteristics often deemed to be relevant.

Also, the theories are not mutually exclusive, i.e., there is some conceptual overlap between the different areas of thought.

While it is our belief that steward leaders most frequently exhibit the characteristics of transformational leadership, they also draw on many elements from other leadership traditions.

If we consider the examples of steward leaders described in this book, post-war stewards like Chung Ju-yung and Konosuke Matsushita – who came from a background of difficulty, with limited education – seem to have had the ability to put the needs of others first, often demonstrating the traits of servant leaders.

During the 1980s and 1990s, a period where much of the world saw rapid growth and major shifts enabled through the IT revolution and globalization, steward leaders exhibited many of the characteristics of adaptive leadership (for example Ratan Tata and Stan Shih). Fast-forward to 2015 and many of our steward leaders have

Table 7.1   Leadership thinking relevant to stewardship

Theory	Key characteristics
Transactional	• **Contingent reward**: Contracts exchange of rewards for effort, promises rewards for good performance, recognizes accomplishments • **Management by exception (active)**: Watches and searches for deviations from rules and standards, takes corrective action • **Management by exception (passive)**: Intervenes only if standards are not met • **Laissez-faire**: Abdicates responsibility, avoids making decisions
Transformational	• **Charisma:** Provides vision & sense of mission, instills pride, gains respect and trust • **Inspiration**: Communicates high expectations, uses symbols to focus efforts, expresses important purposes in simple ways • **Intellectual stimulation**: Promotes intelligence, rationality, and careful problem solving • **Individualized consideration**: Gives personal attention, treats each employee individually, coaches and advises
Servant	Putting the needs of others first through: • **Listening**: Emphasizing the importance of communication and seeking to identify the will of the people • **Empathy**: Understanding others and accepting them • **Healing:** The ability to help make whole • **Awareness**: Being awake • **Persuasion**: Influencing others using arguments not power • **Conceptualization**: Thinking beyond the present-day need and stretching it into a possible future • **Foresight**: Foreseeing outcomes of situations • **Stewardship**: Holding something in trust, serving the needs of others • **Commitment** to the growth of people • **Building community**: Building cohesion and unity for common goals
Authentic	Owning one's personal experiences and behaving in accordance with one's true self through: • Self-awareness • Relational transparency • Internalized moral perspective • Balanced processing
Adaptive	Interpretation of data is key to building adaptive organizational culture by: • **Diagnosing** the system, challenges, and political landscape • **Acting politically**: expanding informal authority, finding allies, staying connected to the opposition, managing authority, staying accountable, and encouraging dissent • **Orchestrating** the conflict • **Building an adaptive culture** through shared responsibility, encouraging independent judgment, developing leadership capacity, and creating a learning organization

(*continued*)

Table 7.1   (*Continued*)

Theory	Key characteristics
Shared Leadership	Leadership is a collective social process that does not rely on one person – and in fact it cannot if the group is to be successful. The purpose of a leader is to make sure there is leadership to ensure that all four dimensions of leadership are being addressed: 1. A shared, motivating group purpose or vision 2. Action, progress, and results 3. Collective unity or team spirit 4. Attention to individuals
Transcendent Leadership	Leadership of the self is important and requires: • **Self-awareness** through reflection and introspection, allowing leaders to achieve clarity regarding core values and mental models and how these shaped decisions • **Self-regulation** whereby leader aligns his/her values with intentions and actions (e.g., transparency of motives, goals, and values; leading by example)

embraced notions of shared leadership – sometimes referred to as distributed or invisible leadership. For example Zhang Ruimin and Lee Kum Kee are proponents of cascading leadership down, so that each employee has leadership responsibility. As such, the leadership style of steward leaders adapts to the circumstances dictated by their individual context.

Is leadership culturally specific? Do we need to consider the cultural context in which leadership is occurring and adapt steward leadership accordingly? While this may be true, and it is certain that there are norms and values that vary in importance in different cultures, we believe that steward leaders demonstrate the three universal characteristics we have outlined, independent of their cultural context.

However, there may be certain environments that are more receptive and conducive to steward leaders than others.

In pursuing long-term organizational wealth, leadership rises to the level of stewardship when leaders not only succeed in their mission but also seek to optimize the best interests of society, for all stakeholders, not just shareholders.[8]

Steward leaders recognize that stakeholder interests may not always be aligned; their role is to balance these in a manner that creates value not just for the organization but for societal stakeholders, too. This requires an inspired insight and vision, reinforced by an unwavering commitment to excellence and the ability to find a "middle way" that keeps competing interests in mind when making decisions.[9]

At the organizational level, leaders do this by building trust in employees, which elicits a sense of personal ownership. Trust is a key building block for any free enterprise system, as it reduces transaction costs and facilitates collective action among societal stakeholders, which is beneficial for all.[10] Trust is an emotional attribute that steward leaders need to earn and continue to build via consistent and reliable performance and integrity.

The above traits appear somewhat contrary to what is expounded by economic models of human behavior and theories of organizational economics, which assume that an individual's behavior is opportunistic, self-serving, and motivated by satisfying personal goals.[11] The nature of some of these qualities also makes them difficult to assess in real time and they are best studied retrospectively. In addition, stewardship goes beyond the values of individuals to encompass their experiences, exposure, and reputation.

We examined the examples of strong steward leaders in the first chapter – those individuals held up as extraordinary not only in terms of their ability to drive superior value creation over time for the companies entrusted to their care, but also in terms of their contribution to the societies in which they operate. Using our empirical study, we identified key terms and classified the words that emerged, and then mapped them on to leadership attributes that emerged as common among steward leaders.

Steward leaders lead with impact and ensure that their organizations foster positive relationships with stakeholders both internally and externally. They safeguard the organization's future and ensure that it and its stakeholders thrive over the long term. And they drive social good, behaving in a way that is accountable and responsible. We examine each of these dimensions in turn in Table 7.2.[12]

Leading with Impact

Steward leaders are able to have an unambiguously positive impact on the organizations they lead, characterized by the following observable behaviors:

- Equity
- Reputation

Table 7.2   Dimensions of steward leader behaviors

Attributes	Dimensions	Faculty
Leading with impact	Influence	• Mobilizes stakeholders around a compelling vision • Drives social and economic impact (e.g., thought leadership, business success) • Inspiring in character
	Contextual intelligence	• Aware of individual strengths and weaknesses; willing to learn from others • Sensitizes oneself to needs of others and cultural differences • Successfully seeks consensus among disparate stakeholders • Willing to engage in transformative efforts
	Commitment	• Possesses drive (tenacity, energy, initiative) • Acts conscientiously • Executes quality communication with the stakeholders
	Reputation	• Achieves ubiquitous trust • Realizes consistency in actions • Strives for authenticity • Acts courageously in face of adversity
	Equity	• Ensures that rewards are distributed in a way that corresponds to contribution rather than power
Safeguarding the future	Prudence	• Employs a measured approach to risk • Effectively combines short-term planning with long-term thinking • Pursues caution in practical affairs
	Care	• Protects the interests of the stakeholders • Encourages strong forward-looking policies and standards • Implements careful management of resources
Driving social good	Accountability	• Adheres to moral and ethical principles • Delivers responsible decision-making • Encourages openness and transparency
	Compassion	• Displays and exercises empathy

Source: Summary of Literature: Effective Stewardship. (2014).Stewardship Asia Centre & IMD. Singapore. Retrieved from http://www.stewardshipasia.com.sg/knowledge/effective_stewardship.pdf

- Commitment
- Contextual intelligence
- Influence.

Equity

Steward leaders are meritocratic. By ensuring that rewards (not just financial, but also additional opportunities and development activities) are distributed in a way that corresponds to contribution rather than power, steward leaders send a clear message that it is performance that determines progress within the company.

Our empirical study confirms the importance of these values to the very fabric of well-stewarded companies, as reported in their narratives. Companies ranking highly on our Implied Stewardship Index demonstrated accountability and responsibility with their greater use of personal pronouns and other personal references in their 10-K statements. In contrast, companies that ranked lower on our implied stewardship index avoided personal pronouns, which creates a sense of removal of management from operations.

While the potentially higher ranking companies emphasized their connection to their environment through a focus on sustainability and contribution to society, there was a scarcity of such words in the potentially lower ranking companies. They clearly state that their results have been audited and that they represent a true and fair view of the state of the company's performance. Potentially lower ranking companies are more likely to use "unaudited" reports, and are more reticent when it comes to describing their governance codes and practices.

Reputation

Through integrity of words and action, the steward leader strives for authenticity, delivers on commitments, and cultivates trust. His or her ability to act courageously in the face of adversity builds a sense of safety within the organization.

Fifteen days after becoming chairman of the Tata group, Ratan Tata faced an issue with a union member in Tata Motors, who had about 200 disruptive, violent, intimidating followers. While there was great pressure on Ratan Tata to appease him to get him out of the way, Ratan Tata refused. He describes the situation: "He beat up or arranged to beat up four to five hundred of our employees. The police were in his pocket. You could go to the police and chances were that nothing would happen. And then he emerged on a really nasty path of going to our officers' homes at two in the morning, ringing the bell with ski caps on, and then stabbing them, always in the thigh so they didn't die but they all had to go get surgery. So he demoralized the management."

A strike was then called and production halted. Ratan Tata put out a call to the workers to return to work. Since the workers were afraid of what this person would do, he decided to go and stay in the plant for three days with them when they began returning to work. Production restarted. Finally the police stepped in and arrested the individual, ending the strike. Upon his release from prison, a contract was put out on Ratan Tata's life. Again, everybody said, "Why don't you make up with him?" We never did, and that was the turning point of labor relations for that company. Looking back on it, I would never have done it any other way.

Thomas Gilbane Jr is the CEO of US construction company Gilbane, a family company that has been in business for 140 years. He is the great-great-grandson of founder William Gilbane; in describing the legacy of reputation and integrity within the company, he sums up the importance that steward leaders attach to reputation: "As young children my father taught us the importance of integrity above all else. He was fond of saying that a person's reputation is their legacy – taking years to build and only minutes to destroy."

Commitment

Imbued with tenacity, energy, and a willingness to take initiative, steward leaders are highly driven and dedicated to achievement.[13] They act conscientiously and execute quality communication with stakeholders. As described in a previous chapter, leaders recognize that communicating is fundamental to their ability to convey their vision to others. At BMW, Norbert Reithofer has been able to garner union support for the tough decisions he has taken – for example, cutting 8100 jobs in 2008. This is remarkable given that German unions are notoriously tough negotiators when it comes to job cuts. Reithofer's conviction that any car maker that wants to succeed in the 21st century needs success that self-sustains, and his ability to communicate that hard message to multiple audiences has enabled him to retain widespread support.

We can learn a great deal about commitment from Masamoto Yashiro, who was brought in to turn around Long-Term Credit Bank of Japan, a failed industrial lender that had been rescued by the Japanese government and later sold for about $1 billion. In order to engineer a successful turnaround, Yashiro, by his own admission, "didn't do things the Japanese way."[14] He faced up to the reality that a decade of stagnation, producing virtually zero interest rates, had fundamentally altered the needs, demands, and risk appetites of the bank's clients. He set about restructuring the bank, now rebranded as Shinsei ("new life"), into a more vibrant, consumer-friendly business that would put the customer first. In addition to new classes of consumer products, Shinsei started offering loan securitization services as well as merger-and-acquisition advice for middle-sized companies.

Within a few years, the bank's retail business was growing at an annual rate of 35–40 percent, and income from commissions and fees had risen from 15 percent in 2000 to 65–70 percent.[15] In bringing about these achievements, Yashiro had to dispel criticism from those who were convinced that Shinsei's new owners were vulture funds only looking for short-term profit. Some opposition went as far as branding him a "national enemy."[16] But the results spoke for themselves, and Shinsei became known worldwide as one of the most dramatic business turnarounds in Japan's corporate history. By bringing in new ways of making money in retail banking and corporate financing, and engineering the bank turnaround through innovation and having the courage to stand up to critics and politicians, Yashiro demonstrated the commitment required to act courageously in the face of harsh criticism and adversity.

Contextual intelligence

Steward leaders demonstrate profound understanding of their own strengths and weaknesses – and a willingness to proactively manage shortcomings. They are empathetic, showing concern for the needs of others, and demonstrate a respect for cultural nuances. This awareness and respect for disparate viewpoints and contexts allows them to successfully seek consensus among stakeholders. Their desire to seek out and understand diverse viewpoints also helps them build contextual understanding, from which they can successfully understand the needs of all involved and initiate transformative efforts that address these.

John Chambers, CEO of Cisco Systems, has developed a reputation for impressive contextual intelligence – for example predicting that voice transmission would become free long before computer networks could even carry it. How does he develop his ability to sense trends ahead of the crowd? By listening closely to customers and employees; in this way, he seeks to understand social, economic, or technological trends that signal major shifts. In order to institutionalize this, Chambers introduced a collaborative decision-making model that allows Cisco to track such signals and respond swiftly to them, in order to rapidly commercialize new opportunities quickly.

Influence

Through their ability to articulate a vision that is meaningful for all stakeholders, steward leaders convey the corporate purpose consistently to them. This clarity helps build understanding of integrity between action and mission, and the distinct value that the company contributes across all spheres. For employees, this means they understand how their actions are linked with the company's overall mission, which is an energizing employment proposition. Research has shown that purpose is one of the key drivers of motivation. Investors who are able to understand the leader's vision and how it connects to long-term growth opportunities are more likely to develop a sense of ownership and connection with the corporate purpose.

For shareholders and investors, steward leaders have a clear focus and the ability to proactively leverage growth opportunities (through new products or markets, or new business models) and business efficiency ensures they deliver good and sustainable business results. Top- and bottom-line growth is a key objective – just not at the expense of other priorities.

For family business Mars, established in 1911 in the US with an articulated purpose of creating "mutuality of benefits for all stakeholders," financial impact remains the priority – but not at the expense of everything else. In the words of Pamela Mars-Wright, the priority is clear: "Don't get me wrong. We're very competitive. We want to win. We want to beat our competition. Absolutely, but at the expense of everything else? Absolutely not. Doing things simply because they are going to return to us more money? No. It's more about doing it because we love what we do and we're passionate about it and it's fun."[17]

Steward leaders are also deeply concerned with managing risk – including financial risk. We discussed this earlier, in examining greater financial conservatism in well-stewarded companies and their tendency to prefer lower financial leverage. When we compare the word usage related to finances, it is interesting to note that companies who score highly on our Implied Stewardship Index were more likely to use words such as *budget, capex, cash flow, EBIT, margin, overheads, profit, reinvested,* and *revenue.* This is distinct from words used more frequently in lower-scoring companies, including *bankruptcy, creditors, debt, defaults, loan, repay,* and *solvency.* (For more details, refer to the Appendix.)

For customers, their ability to frame a relevant proposition ensures that steward leaders deliver on their promise. The ability to build in a positive social contribution to the corporate purpose and to communicate this to societal stakeholder concerns helps to build a sense of connection in the broader community. Steward leaders have an ability to deliver this message in a way that inspires and energizes stakeholders around their vision.

Safeguarding the Future

Stewards have the ability to be in touch with operational reality, while simultaneously extracting themselves sufficiently to take a top-level view. By scanning social media and talking to competitors and actors from radically different industries and activities, steward leaders retain a combination of mental flexibility combined with an awareness of what lies beyond the horizon. Different leaders have different techniques for combining short- and long-term perspective, in order to fill in their peripheral vision and maximize their capability to detect vulnerability and blind spots, while maintaining a clear eye on the long-term forces of change.

As such, stewards have the ability to balance "sprints and marathons."[18] By exploring the strategic and tactical priorities that are occupying managerial time and attention and how they relate to the future opportunities, steward leaders pay attention to allocating resources to balance these two priorities – making adjustments where required. The insights derived from our studies appear to confirm this; companies scoring high on the Implied Stewardship Index performed better over the longer term, with a much higher return on invested capital than lower ranking companies.

In considering how the organization will fulfil its purpose, a steward leader engages in a productive working relationship with the board. This includes demonstrating trust and providing board members with relevant information in a timely manner.

Steward leaders demonstrate both prudence and care in their actions – to ensure that the organizational culture is one in which risk is actively managed – and cultivate a healthy and constructive environment for all stakeholders.

The results of our study show that well-stewarded companies describe their businesses with words and phrases that have a long-term orientation. They also emphasize their corporate values, beliefs, and philosophy by using emotional words. In contrast, other companies often use emotional words to blame others and to exaggerate their own performance. This is often inconsistent not only with the numbers but also with the overall tone of their texts and reports. Well-stewarded companies describe their business in positive tones, whereas poorly-stewarded companies will typically describe their business in neutral or negative tones.

Prudence

Steward leaders know how to experiment and take calculated risks, with the intention of finding growth opportunities to build their businesses. They are able to recognize and take advantage of opportunities as they arise. However, they are able to balance this with the need to exercise caution in practical affairs, never gambling with the organization's future. They actively scan the environment to monitor for risks, and have a strategy to manage a range of extreme, unforeseen scenarios that could impact the firm's competitiveness. In this way, they effectively combine short-term planning with long-term thinking.

Our quantitative study findings confirm the notion that steward leaders exercise prudence in balancing risks and opportunities to achieve stable growth over time. For example, if we look at the differences in stock price volatility between companies, those ranking in the lowest quadrant on our Implied Stewardship Index have a significantly higher stock price volatility than companies ranking in the upper quartile. (Refer to Figure A.7 in the Appendix for more details.)

Care

The organizations shaped by steward leaders tend to have corporate cultures that value relationships based on trust, and employees are actively engaged in meaningful corporate purpose over time. These employees have a clear view of their career path within the company, concrete ideas about the possibilities afforded by the company, and an understanding of how they will best be able to contribute their talents and energies to creating company value – as well as how these may be developed in the future. These leaders also consider which organizational structure best fits to build the intrinsic motivation of employees and develop their potential to contribute in the future.

Eiji Toyoda acknowledged the importance of valuing employees and caring for them when he said: "Employees are offering a very important part of their life to us. If we don't use their time effectively, we are wasting their lives."[19]

Zhang Ruimin propelled Haier's international expansion by allowing its workforce to reorganize into hundreds of largely autonomous internal units, with the freedom to select their own leaders and to compete with other units for talent and specialized projects. Additionally, frontline staff can collect ideas from customers and report these to management.

Steward leaders also, by their action and example, ensure "regeneration," inspiring the next generation, to ensure the succession of steward leadership.

There is a marked difference in words that potentially well-stewarded companies use with regard to their purpose and identity; terms appear to be more relational and buoyant – with *align, engage,* and *motivate* appearing. This contrasts with terms used by companies that are potentially poorly stewarded, which more frequently use words like *appraisal, dismiss, evaluate, replaced,* and *uncommitted.* (See the Appendix for more details.)

Driving Social Good

Steward leaders understand the organization's connection to society and the role it plays in delivering meaningful benefits to the wider community. The steward leader understands that profit is the result of delivering benefit to society rather than the objective. Staying in touch with stakeholders' expectations of the company and managing the gap between their expectations is required to build understanding and trust. They also demonstrate clear accountability and compassion in the way they view the organization's role in society.

If we consider words related to different stakeholders by potentially well-stewarded companies (*academic, children, cities, education, human, locally, marketplace, owners, parent, youth, etc.*), there is a striking distinction from words used by companies that are potentially poorly stewarded, where there is a greater incidence of words related to litigation (*appeal, attorney, claims, defendant, indemnification, litigation, settlements, suit, etc.*).

Ratan Tata articulated his vision for India in the global economy, and the role that Tata could play in enabling this to become a reality: "The vision I have for India in the next decade is of a nation with vastly improved connectivity in communications providing education, personal interaction, e-commerce, and telephony contact for the overwhelming mass of its people. I see our country being connected through major highway networks, thus shrinking the time required to move goods to the marketplace. I see our consumers exercising an unprecedented degree of choice, with the Indian marketplace becoming a vibrantly competitive arena, fully integrated with the world. Equally, I foresee that the ambitions of the Indian entrepreneur will not be confined to domestic boundaries and our immensely valuable human capital will leave its mark on the global marketplace."[20]

With an integrated view of their firm's contribution to social good, steward leaders spend time listening to external stakeholders. These include customers and suppliers, as well as governmental agencies, non-governmental organizations, unions, and other civil society actors.

Conversations with a wide variety of stakeholders to "stay in touch" and to remain accessible, combined with the ability to listen and really hear their concerns, build both trust and awareness of concerns. This sensitizes leaders to their potential impact and where they can make a real impact – either positive or negative. They do not view this as Corporate Social Responsibility (CSR) or as an activity that is separate from their business – a philanthropic activity to be farmed out to their charitable foundation.

"I don't really like the word philanthropy. I consider it more a matter of building trust in the community. It means working with a broader constituency than those who buy your products and services.

It involves building good will," said Jaime Zóbel de Ayala, chairman and CEO of the Ayala Corporation.[21] Steward leaders view driving social good as central to their – and their firm's – purpose, not as a peripheral activity.

Masami Yamamoto is the president of Fujitsu, the world's fourth largest IT services provider, and its second oldest, founded in 1935. Yamamoto describes how the company creates value by integrating technology into people's everyday lives and businesses.

"By applying the innovation of supercomputers in a variety of fields, we believe we can contribute to the creation of a prosperous society. Together with our customers, we are striving to contribute to a more prosperous society. A more prosperous society means people having a more secure and sustainable lifestyle. We would like to use ICT capabilities for the benefit of society. This is made possible by supercomputers. It will help us to develop new ways of thinking and new solutions to shape a better tomorrow."[22]

A number of Asian business leaders have demonstrated stewardship in how they have led their firms and the impact they have had on the societies in which they operate. Our intention here is not to glorify a particular leader or culture as better at stewardship than another, but rather to stimulate learning and exchange across contexts.

Accountability

In strictly and absolutely adhering to moral and ethical principles, and behaving in a way that is irreproachable from an integrity standpoint, steward leaders send a strong message to society and contribute to cultivating an environment in which this is the expectation and the norm. This strong moral and ethical stance reinforces their ability to make decisions that are responsible in that they take into account the impact on all stakeholders. They encourage openness and transparency, which reinforces their willingness to be held accountable.

Compassion

Steward leaders show empathy and compassion. Their actions demonstrate awareness of the degree of interdependence between business and society in terms of resources and talent. Through understanding the needs of others, and where possible helping to address those needs, steward leaders build the connections and ties with other societal actors, playing their part in making a positive impact.

They treat their employees as valued members of the company. The focus of Konosuke Matsushita on his people was fundamental. "We produce people, and we also produce electrical goods," he observed – in that order. He believed that the growth of a company's employees was essential to a business's success; business, first and foremost, was about cultivating human potential. In addition to cultivating employees' technical skills and knowledge, Matsushita believed in the importance of cultivating individual self-reliance and responsibility in order to help employees understand the value and significance of their own work and of the obligation of the company to contribute to society.

Our study findings confirm the importance placed on their relationships with internal and external stakeholders by companies ranking more highly on the Implied Stewardship Index. The results show that these companies consider their employees as valuable long-term assets, while poorly-stewarded companies treat their employees as replaceable or disposable. The more highly ranked companies also enhance and deliver value to customers, while poorly-stewarded companies under-play the importance and veracity of customer complaints. Finally, while well-stewarded companies build long-term rapport with a range of stakeholders, poorly-stewarded companies are haunted by lawsuits from disgruntled parties.

What Drives Steward Leaders?

While the above describes what we observe when we see steward leaders behaving or doing, what is it that drives their behavior? What are the capabilities that prompt them to behave in this way? Again, while every individual leader is different and personality differences may explain some specific abilities or sensitivities, we wish to highlight some of the key elements that we see as distinctive.

Individual congruence

Steward leaders combine their strong sense of mission with the state of congruence. Congruence is the ability to reflect on how you explain events – and what they mean – as they occur, and to compare this with your vision of how things should be in an ideal world. Key to this process of making sense is the ability to reflect. Exploring and considering the gap helps leaders to seek information to fill those gaps.

Steward leaders take the time they need to reflect, individually and with trusted members of their team, before the gap becomes too big.

In this way, steward leaders engage in a process of continuous learning and development.[23] In addition to taking a conscious look at actions and events, they consider emotions, experiences, and responses, and use that information to add to their existing knowledge base to reach a higher level of understanding.

Fostering learning and dialogue

Steward leaders combine an ability to influence with their inspiring message, while staying in inquiry mode.[24] This ability to simultaneously transmit and absorb helps them to stay in touch with reality, while energizing others with their message and empowering them with clear information. By being willing to engage in the "grit" of the organizational work through sharing control as well as participating in design and execution, steward leaders stay firmly grounded in the company's day-to-day activities. They gather data and test hypotheses in a very direct way.

Also, by fostering an environment that allows learning and dialogue, steward leaders help to surface conflicting views and stimulate honest and informed exchange. This helps to build learning at the organizational level while contributing to productive relationships and freedom of choice.[25]

Employees who are learning and empowered are sensitive to signals, question assumptions, and shift course when needed. This helps to build organizational adaptability. Stan Shih used "reverse thinking" to question existing processes within Acer. Ratan Tata is known to say "question the unquestionable" to encourage challenging assumptions.

Often steward leaders are independent thinkers who have the agility to build organizational adaptability. Masamoto Yashiro was an "outsider" when he was recruited to take over as CEO of Shinsei Bank, and he successfully engineered a business transformation by challenging rather than upholding traditional Japanese business philosophy.

Creating a shared reality

Steward leaders are able to communicate their view of the big picture to others to build a shared vision of the current reality. They paint a compelling picture of the road to achieve that purpose. By connecting to this understanding of how they are contributing to something bigger, employees feel empowered. They believe that their contribution makes a difference.

Peter Senge stresses the importance of the leader's role in interpreting reality for employees: "Much of the leverage leaders can actually exert lies in helping people achieve more accurate, more insightful and more empowering views of reality."[26] Creating meaning is a powerful way to mobilize stakeholder energy and commitment.

A key component of this is seeking feedback from employees directly on how purpose is translating into reality and then doing something about it. For Mars, its five principles – quality, responsibility, mutuality, efficiency, and freedom – are core to its business. Or so it thought. When Mars conducted an employee survey, the results showed that its principles were not perceived as being put into reality: "The survey came back and basically it was horrible. It was a wake-up call," said Pamela Mars-Wright. "We weren't falling apart at the seams or anything like that, but what was evident was that we weren't living the five principles. We weren't the company we thought. We weren't the company our associates thought we were. We weren't living the five principles. So, they were five words up on a wall. Everybody could repeat them … It's not that complicated, but we weren't living them. So, we decided, to go back to the five principles and to really focus on them."

At the organizational level

Steward leaders are also architects of organizations designed to fulfil their purpose and role. They do this by building an environment of trust. They provide sufficient structure to allow for decision-making anchored in firm values and purpose. This is balanced with enough flexibility to provide empowerment and autonomy so that motivation and energy are unleashed.

For many, a decentralized structure is a key enabler for empowering people and allowing efficient flows of information. Globalization and its steady erosion of boundaries have made this more relevant than ever before.

Samuel Palmisano had a long career in IBM, and as COO he led its outsourcing business. He served as the company's CEO from 2002 to 2012, and as its chairman until 2012. He has received many public accolades for his ability to elevate IBM's operational excellence as well as for creating and leading IBM's Global Services business unit. In 2006, he described the implication of globalization on organizations when he wrote: "Hierarchical, command and control structures simply do not work anymore. They impede information flows inside companies, hampering the fluid and collaborative nature of work today."[27]

Embedding values into operational decision-making is required to hold the organization true to its purpose on a daily basis. This requires clear practical translation of values into operations and to guide decision-making.

Building the resilience and adaptability needed to shift course when threats and opportunities arise as well as a keen ability to scan and diagnose relevant data are critical to survive and thrive over the long term. Organizations need to have the capability to comprehensively and effectively scan the external environment to detect, filter, and understand the importance of signals in order to understand what is coming next.

Collecting correct and relevant data is critical. Information needs to be available and transparent internally. In addition, there needs to be clear accountability and recognition of performance. This helps build the sense among employees that individual contributions make a difference, and that they are visible and fairly evaluated. This contributes to a sense of collective responsibility for the performance of the organization, nurturing a virtuous circle of empowerment. In the words of Kiichiro Toyoda: "Each person thoroughly fulfilling their duties generates great power that, gathered together in a chain, creates a ring of power."[28]

Most corporate cultures are not only resistant to learning but actively discourage it. In such cultures, employees are rewarded to the extent to which they espouse the views of senior management. Toeing the party line pays. Difficult questions about the company's future are often left unasked – and therefore have no chance of being answered.

It took a long time for employees to internalize Ratan Tata's mantra, despite his frequent repetition to "question the unquestionable." He impressed upon younger managers the importance of not accepting things just because that was the way it had been done in the past, repeating "Don't just accept something as a holy cow. Go question it." However, he encountered resistance on the part of senior managers who told the younger ones: "Look young man, don't question me."[29]

Peter Senge writes that team learning starts with dialogue, the capacity of members of a team to suspend assumptions and enter into genuine thinking together.[30] Learning organizations reward employees based on the quality of the questions they ask; they value assumptions being challenged.

When Minoru Makihara took the reins of Mitsubishi Corporation in 1992, he introduced an open door policy – a revolutionary idea among Japanese executives. His rationale? "The CEO has to elicit ideas by talking to employees at every level of the organization," he observed.[31]

Many organizations have a culture in which people attempt to solve problems without questioning assumptions to identify root causes. Organizations with a learning culture cultivate inquiry. This recognizes that the way a problem is defined and solved can be the source of the problem. A core capability for building a resilient, learning organization is the ability to ask better questions.

A learning culture emphasizes common goals and mutual influence, encourages open communication, and allows for publicly testing assumptions and beliefs. Toyota championed incremental learning and used smaller-scale achievements as testing grounds for global initiatives. For example, Eiji Toyoda created a learning culture that fostered inquiry and re-framing problems. Employees were encouraged to identify root causes and to develop countermeasures.

They used a method called the "Five Whys," which entails asking "why?" five times (see Figure 7.1) to understand the underlying causes of a problem.

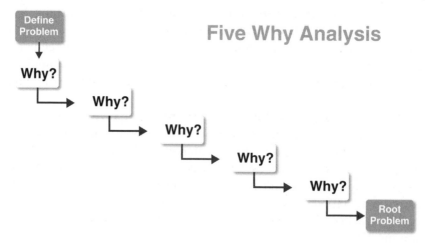

Figure 7.1   The Five Whys

This iterative question-asking method serves to clarify the cause and effect of problems in order to determine the underlying root cause. A central part of Toyota's corporate DNA is responsibility and the importance of reflecting on mistakes and coming up with ways to address weaknesses (*hansei*). According to Toyota's Tooru Matsubara: "At Toyota, we expect every assembly line worker to direct their wisdom toward originating ideas for improving base costs, quality, and safety."[32] As such, the line manager's role was to foster an atmosphere in which line workers felt empowered to express their suggestions, and felt supported to implement these.

Measuring Individual Progress

Individual steward leaders have very different personalities and ways of behaving. What they share is their ability to use their strong personal conviction to drive and sustain organizational purpose and culture to enable decision-making and activity that is consistent and aligned, together with a clear investment in nurturing high quality connections both internally and externally, demonstrating their understanding of the firm's integral role in society. The relationships between these spheres are represented in Figure 7.2.

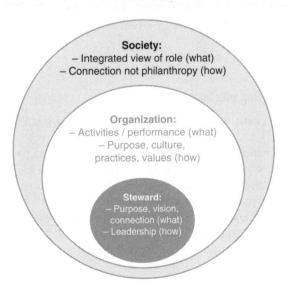

Figure 7.2   Steward Leadership Spheres

If it is your aspiration to be a steward for your organization, we encourage you to answer the questionnaire in the box below. This will help you to identify strengths as well as opportunities to help secure your individual and organizational legacy.

Refer to the following box and reflect upon what your score may be telling you about where you can lever strengths, and what critical areas may be creating areas of vulnerability.

Then answer the following:

- What characteristics do you wish to develop in order to build a learning organization that is adaptable and resilient over the long term?
- How can you ensure that your internal talent is committed and inspired to build the organizational future?
- How can you ensure that your shareholders and investors understand what you are trying to achieve and support you in doing so?

What areas do you need to develop to move from leader to steward?

(Scale: 1 to 7, 1 = Strongly disagree, 5 = Neither agree nor disagree, 7 = Strongly agree)
    See Table 7.3 for scoring.

Section 1: Leading with impact

1. We have a clear and compelling organizational purpose that all can articulate concisely.
2. I am committed to inspiring and enabling my employees to contribute to the maximum of their ability, and to develop their ability to do so.
3. We have a process in place to transform the emerging visions from all levels of the enterprise to become a shared vision.
4. We invite employees to learn what is going on at every level of the organization to understand how their actions influence others.
5. There is mutual respect in the way people talk to each other and work together across levels and functions.

6. We have forums where employees are encouraged to question assumptions.
7. People feel free to take risks and experiment. There is strong tolerance for failure.

Sections 2: Safeguarding the future

1. I have a clear vision for where I would like the organization to be in 10 years, 20 years, and 50 years.
2. I am satisfied that every individual in the organization is enhancing his or her capacity to create value for the organization.
3. I am satisfied with the degree of dialogue and the quality of questions that are asked by the management team.
4. The board and management have highly qualified members and healthy dynamics to ensure responsible and active oversight.
5. The board has identified a pool of high quality candidates for CEO succession.
6. We have regular and transparent communication with shareholders, investors, and owners.
7. All of our large shareholders and investors exhibit an understanding of our purpose and business.

Section 3: Driving social good

1. I have a firm conviction that my organization is doing something that matters – to me personally and to the larger world.
2. We regularly map the concerns of our stakeholders and discuss the implications with the management team and board.
3. We regularly meet with a wide variety of stakeholders in an open and transparent forum, and have a good understanding of their concerns.
4. The quality of communication both to and from all of our stakeholders is high.
5. I deeply value the trust that is placed in me by all of the firm's stakeholders to play our role responsibly in society.
6. The organization has a net positive impact on the social context in which it operates.
7. We are continually monitoring our impact and trying to improve it.

(continued)

Table 7.3   Stewardship Leadership Scoring

Your Total Score	
21–62	I have some serious concerns about the way our company is addressing long-term value creation, through its leadership and/or its relationship with its societal stakeholders.
63–104	Our company is on the path to stewardship, but needs to address some key challenges and develop additional capabilities to accelerate its transition.
105–147	I am confident that our company will weather current and future challenges to deliver value for all of society.
Section 1 Score	
7–21	Our leadership is failing to create a culture that inspires employees to take ownership and commit to creating a positive impact.
22–35	We have strong points in our leadership, but need to work on strengthening our culture in order to have the impact we seek.
36–49	Our leadership fosters a culture in which employees are empowered to create impact.
Section 2 Score	
7–21	My organization's ability to create sustainable value over the long term is at risk.
22–35	Overall, we are on track to ensure our organization's resilience to deliver value over time, but some key elements need strengthening.
36–49	The high quality of our organization's processes and people ensures that we are taking a long-term view to delivering our mission.
Section 3 Score	
7–21	My company lacks a compelling sense of purpose with regard to its role in society as well as connections with key stakeholders.
22–35	My company seeks to create positive societal impact, but we need to work on how authentically we are doing this and check the strength of our relationships with other societal stakeholders.
36–49	My company's authentic purpose is to create good for all of society and it regularly checks its progress in doing so.

CHAPTER 8

Pitfalls of Stewardship

Dizzying speeds of change continue to accelerate. An ever more connected world is vulnerable to shocks, currency fluctuations, and other forms of volatility. Steward leaders need to steer their organizations through the twists and turns of change. For them and their organizations, reinvention, flexibility, and adaptability are essential. In this environment, staying vigilant about the next threat to competitiveness is critical to securing the viability of organizations. Failing to identify threats can endanger the very survival of the organization and the future of all those involved with it.

In this chapter we will discuss how stewards are vulnerable to certain risks; examine the potential damage; and address risk proactively. The major risks that steward leaders face can be categorized as:

- Reputational
- Behavioral biases
- Leadership transitions
- Leadership feuding
- Political.

Reputational Risk

Reputation is at the heart of the credibility, trust, and confidence inspired by steward leaders. A good reputation is built on past results and bolsters stakeholder confidence in a steward's capability to deliver in the future. Reputation is a testament to a steward's trustworthiness. In some ways, reputation is synonymous with stewardship, an intangible and essential asset for business success.

Great stewards care about reputation, both on the personal and business front. Hong Kong businessman, investor, and philanthropist Li Ka-shing is often quoted as saying: "A good reputation for yourself and your company is an invaluable asset not reflected in the balance sheets."[1] A 2014 survey on global reputation risk reported that 87 percent of the executives rated reputation risk as more important than other strategic risks and 88 percent said their companies were explicitly focusing on managing reputation risk.[2]

Delicate by nature, reputations require vigilant maintenance. Reputation is about external perception, which is continuously assessed by various stakeholders. As a psychological process, perception is highly subjective and easily influenced by sudden events, values, and beliefs. In today's connected environment, reputation is a global issue. A threat to your reputation or that of your organization can come from anywhere. A caustic tweet or a comment on Facebook by a disgruntled employee or bitter customer can have huge repercussions.

There are many less frivolous sources of reputation risk. It may relate to ethics or integrity at any corporate level due to fraud, bribery, and corruption. Another source of risk is from product safety or service issues. Corporate reputation might also be tarnished by a data security breach or a physical security breach. Scandals related to financial reporting and accounting can be even more damaging.

The risks are many and varied; the implications potentially enormous. A challenge to a company's reputation can cause serious damage – resulting in lost sales, higher financing costs, a loss of credibility for the steward leader, and much more.

Longevity is no security against the effects of a destroyed reputation. Consider the case of Arthur Andersen. Founded in 1913, Arthur Andersen was one of the "Big Five" accounting firms.[3] In 2001, one of its clients, Enron, filed for bankruptcy. It was discovered that by means of systematic accounting fraud, Enron had inflated its profits and hidden debts totaling over $1 billion. Consequently, Andersen's performance as an auditor came under intense investigation. The firm was indicted on obstruction of justice charges relating to the firm's handling of the auditing of Enron.

In 2005, the Supreme Court overturned Arthur Andersen's conviction; however, the damage to its reputation was fatal and the firm was all but destroyed. Globally, more than 85,000 employees, most not involved with Enron, lost their jobs. The firm has never filed for bankruptcy and continues to operate a facility mostly used for Accenture training.

"It takes 20 years to build a reputation and five minutes to ruin it. If you think about that, you'll do things differently," said Warren Buffett.[4] He advises business leaders never to do something they would not want to see reported on the front page of their local newspaper. After taking control of Salomon Inc. in the wake of a major 1991 scandal at the financial firm, he famously told a congressional panel that he had a simple message for employees: "Lose money for the firm and I will be understanding; lose a shred of reputation for the firm and I will be ruthless."[5]

So, what do steward leaders do to maintain the reputations of their organizations? Through consistent and constant communication with key stakeholder groups, both internally and externally, a company's reputational asset can be accumulated. Building a reputational asset can become a safety net helping a well-stewarded organization recover quickly from the inevitable challenges to its reputation. If a company has an unblemished reputation, customers, shareholders, and other key stakeholders might give it a second chance.

Toyota, the world's biggest auto company, built sales on a reputation for quality. The company also has numerous initiatives for a better planet and sustainability. From 2009 to 2010, a major recall tarnished its reputation. Akio Toyoda, the founder's grandson, attended a US congressional hearing. At the hearing, Toyoda apologized for allowing the company to put expansion before safety. Choking over his words, Toyoda cried and promised to rethink everything about operations to regain customer confidence.

Toyota's reputation was not finished permanently as widely anticipated. Customers and other key stakeholders did give the company a second chance. Following a sales dip in 2011, the company took the global sales crown from 2012 to 2014. Investing in corporate social responsibility has a real return; it is a strategic investment to establish long-lasting trust with stakeholders.

The most important means of bolstering and maintaining your reputation is to walk the talk. Toyota's story shows that reputation assets must be sustained by continuing proof of excellence – quality products and services, integrity in dealing with stakeholders, safety, and security. Insisting on excellence lies at the heart of great stewardship.

To manage reputation risk effectively, it is essential to identify vulnerable areas that could affect your reputation. Information about vulnerable areas ought to be systematically analyzed; stakeholder expectations ought to be constantly tracked and monitored; reputation impacts ought to be evaluated consistently. When their reputation is in danger, well-stewarded organizations have protocols to guide a professional response from managers.

Risk from Behavioral Biases of Steward Leaders

We all have biases. With the same evidence, people come to different conclusions. We constantly evaluate the world around us – markets, industries, businesses, and people – based on our past experiences. When, as is often the case, our past experiences are limited, behavioral biases can result.

Biases in probability and belief cause us to make bad judgments. For great stewards, this is clearly problematic and damaging. As many decisions are influenced by our subconscious minds, we need to be aware of these biases and correct our thinking to be in line with reality.

Apart from biases in probability and belief, biases in decision-making can negatively affect business and investment decisions. One example is business blind spots, i.e., the tendency not to compensate for one's own cognitive biases. We all have blind spots in one way or another. Great stewards are not immune.

In fact, they might be particularly vulnerable to this risk. It takes decades to build stewardship. But, changes in technology, demographics, and economics may cause dramatic global changes in social institutions and social behaviors.[6] Behaviors, beliefs, and attitudes deeply embedded in the past might not work in the new reality. Failing to keep up with changes might mean that a once great steward no longer leads at the edge. To be a successful steward, we need to be aware that business blind spots are real and hubris could potentially cause us to fail.

Blind spots may be accompanied by overconfidence, which has been defined in three distinct ways:

- Overestimation of one's actual performance
- Over-placement of one's performance relative to others
- Excessive certainty regarding the accuracy of one's beliefs, called over-precision.

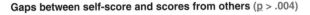

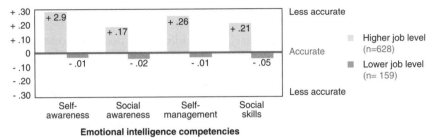

Figure 8.1   Gap in perception of how executives view themselves vs. how others see them

Source: Adapted from Hay Group

The overconfidence effect is a well-established bias. For example, in some tests, people rate their answers as "99 percent certain" but are wrong 40 percent of the time. Overconfidence has been extensively studied in different circumstances. The reality is that people are more certain that they are correct than they have reason to be.

Figure 8.1 illustrates the results of a study showing that the higher up individuals are within an organization, the more likely they are to overrate themselves, and the wider the gap between how they see themselves and how their peers, subordinates, and managers view them.[7]

Overconfidence and business blind spots hinder leadership effectiveness by blocking aspects of reality. When breakthrough ideas do not fit our assumptions and expectations, we may not see the potential value. If we do not expect to see a new reality, we will simply not see it. New ideas may be misunderstood, mocked, or dismissed.

In Asia, after decades of growth and success, a number of companies collapsed during the 1990s Asian financial crisis – including banks and financial institutions. While there were of course many contributing elements, one major factor was overconfidence of local banks. Lending growth surpassed GDP growth in many countries (e.g., Thailand, South Korea, Malaysia) during this period. Despite the warnings raised by some analysts, it was difficult to dampen the firmly entrenched optimism in the region. Another contributing element was the nature of business–government relations in many countries in this region, which has been the subject of much discussion. The notion that moral hazard issuing from state capitalism was any greater in Asia than in any other financial crises before or since, however, has been increasingly challenged. Indeed moral hazard seems to be endemic to capitalism.[8]

Malaysian Airline System (MAS) plausibly provides one such example of overconfidence in the Southeast Asian context. With industry accolades and a five-star rating from Skytrax, MAS appeared full of promising growth potential. Steady growth in demand for Malaysia tourism from new markets such as China, India, Africa, and the Middle East built on this solid foundation. Retroactively, analysts point to a number of factors that undermined its efficiency: poor management, over-reaching on routes, government interference, and unfavorable service and supplier contracts. This led to a series of loss-making years for the company from 2010 onward.

Some studies claim that overconfidence has a bright side. Empirically, overconfidence is associated with greater investment in innovation, improved decision implementation, sufficient risk management, or stimulating entrepreneurship. We would guard against this thinking, as there is a thin line between confidence and overconfidence. Therefore, we need to be careful when people make statements that they could mathematically differentiate the two. Self-confidence based on a strong faith will enable us to reach overarching goals. In contrast, overconfidence without humility and a sense of perspective will lead to mistakes and failures.

Behavior biases destroy value. In distorting their perception, behavioral biases obstruct steward leaders' vision of reality. This can cause a great deal of damage – as was the case with Henry Ford. He was an industrial genius who revolutionized the way we live. However, after 1910, he became increasingly anti-Semitic, anti-immigrant, anti-labor, and anti-liquor. In 1919, he bought a newspaper, *The Dearborn Independent*, to present his views. Ford[9] suffered from many behavior biases, anchoring, conjunction fallacy, and illusory correlation, etc.

In 1920, Ford began publishing a series of articles claiming there was a vast Jewish conspiracy that was the source of the social ills in the United States, including financial scandals and the agricultural depression. The series ran in the following 91 issues. Binding the articles into four volumes titled *The International Jew*, Ford distributed half a million copies to his network of dealerships and subscribers – which was expansive. Its anti-Semitic stance was unambiguous from the beginning, as demonstrated by the front page headline of the

May 22, 1920 issue: "The International Jew: The World's Problem." The text beneath it quoted the New International Encyclopedia as stating: "Among the distinguishing mental and moral traits of the Jews may be mentioned: distaste for hard or violent physical labor; a strong family sense and philoprogenitiveness; a marked religious instinct; the courage of the prophet and martyr rather than of the pioneer and soldier; remarkable power to survive in adverse environments, combined with great ability to retain racial solidarity; capacity for exploitation, both individual and social; shrewdness and astuteness in speculation and money matters generally; an Oriental love of display and a full appreciation of the power and pleasure of social position; a very high average of intellectual ability."[10]

As a prominent business leader – and one of the most famous men in the United States at the time – Henry Ford legitimized ideas that otherwise might not have had the degree of visibility they had with his active support.

Henry Ford's anti-Semitic views damaged his own car business when Jewish leaders called for a boycott of Ford cars. During this period, Ford was sued for libel and the case went to trial. It seemed that Ford was afraid of slumping sales and he decided to settle the libel case out of court. In 1927, Ford closed the newspaper, acknowledged errors, and asked publicly for forgiveness.

Business blind spots may cloud our perception of a new trend in the market and, consequently, risk the future of an otherwise well-stewarded organization or an established industry. Consider the Quartz Crisis (also known as the Quartz Revolution), the classic story of the dramatic changes in the Swiss watch-making industry in the 1970s and early 1980s.

The Swiss watch industry prospered after WWII, as the activities of its competitors were disrupted by wartime. Prior to the 1970s, the Swiss watch industry had nearly 65 percent of the world watch market. In 1954, Swiss engineer Max Hetzel developed an electronic wristwatch called Accutron. It was dismissed outright by the Swiss watch industry; in their view the quality of quartz watches was inferior. They chose to focus on traditional mechanical watches, confident that these would continue to dominate the market.

Asian companies embraced the new quartz technology and soon began fulfilling an unmet market demand for inexpensive watches. The Japanese watch maker, Seiko, introduced the first commercially viable quartz watch, the Seiko Quartz Astron 35SQ.

Over the next 10 years, the Japanese Quartz Revolution pushed the Swiss watch market into freefall – it declined to less than 10 percent of the world watch market. By 1983, 1000 Swiss watchmakers had disappeared. Only 600 remained and they were struggling severely. Between 1970 and 1988, Swiss watch employment fell from 90,000 to 28,000. All of this was thanks to a blind spot.

The Swiss watch industry was in turmoil. Two large watch firms – ASUAG and SSIH – were facing liquidation. Nicolas Hayek, a Zurich-based consultant, was brought in to effect turnarounds. Hayek merged the two companies, renamed the company the Swatch Group, and introduced a cheap Swatch watch to compete head on with the Japanese. The Swatch watch was a success. In fact, Hayek subsequently took over many luxury watch brands and built them up.[11] The Swiss watch industry regained its leading position, and Hayek has been credited with saving the Swiss watch industry.

Many view the entry of Apple, Huawei, and other technology firms into the wearable market as a new threat to the Swiss watch industry. "I do expect an Ice Age coming toward us ... So far I see watchmakers in this country making the same mistakes as back then," Elmar Mock, Swatch co-inventor, said. "We've seen a lot of arrogance in the Swiss watch industry in the past few years, calling the smartwatch a gadget and not taking it seriously." Critics of the Apple watch include Swatch Group CEO Nick Hayek (son of Nicolas Hayek) who does not "believe [smartwatches] are the next revolution."[12] Whose prediction will ultimately prove correct?

The example of the Swiss watch industry in the 1970s is not an isolated case. Many companies have been left behind by disruptive technologies. From 1885 to 2013, the Dow Jones Industrial Average (DJIA)'s components changed 53 times. Many big names have been dropped from the DJIA in recent shakeups, including Kodak, GM, and Alcoa. What do they have in common? While their individual circumstances differ, they all failed to see the big picture, i.e., they suffered from major business blind spots.

The reality is that behavior biases can derail the growth and profitability of previously well-stewarded organizations. To succeed as a steward, we need to learn how to recognize our behavior biases and work on areas of weakness. Behavior biases can be avoided. Li Ka-shing says: "The art of good management lies in the capacity to accept change, and the ability to meld new and traditional thinking."[13]

Research by Hay suggests that senior leaders often lose touch with those they lead. Many successful executives are victims of their own success, believing their own hype. Due to ego, over-confidence, or lack of honest feedback, many work in ever increasing isolation.

At the top in their organizations, great stewards need to develop their own self-awareness. Developing humility and self-awareness is helpful in considering what worked in the past – and yet might not work in the future. Reflecting upon their failures, as well the failures of others, is critical to avoiding the hubris that has tripped up otherwise great leaders. What lessons could you learn from your failures and those of others? This requires staying open to learning, remaining humble, and continuing to seek feedback in order to build an accurate perception of yourself.

A high-school dropout, Li Ka-shing recounts his teenage years: "Without the money for new books I bought old ones, textbooks used by teachers for high school. I only had a dictionary and the books and I studied on my own. When I was done with the books, I exchanged them for more old books. In the circumstances then, I was working for a future. ... While other people learned, I grabbed knowledge."[14]

Complacent leaders tend to shut out new ideas and knowledge. Once they become convinced of their worldview and shut out other perspectives, they are no longer challenging and inspiring. Often, they begin to resist change, or are slow to anticipate the need to change. They then begin to lose their competitive edge, lagging behind competition, or stop responding to innovations.

Steward leaders make learning a lifelong process, broadening their perspectives and eroding behavior biases. That is why even in his late eighties, Li Ka-shing tries daily to read books about science, economics, politics, and philosophy. And as Warren Buffett's business partner, Charlie Munger, revealed: "The other big secret is that we're good at lifelong learning. Warren is better in his seventies and eighties, in many ways, than he was when he was younger. If you keep learning all the time, you have a wonderful advantage." Learning can identify obsolete ideas and assumptions, and prompt ideas for re-imagining ways of doing and thinking.

To anticipate how businesses will need to re-invent themselves in the future, great stewards "grab" knowledge – like Li Ka-shing. Great stewards keep learning, anticipate changes in culture and the economy, and inspire employees to embrace new thoughts and technology breakthroughs. They are the ones who will thrive and pass on their legacies to the next generations of stewards.

Great stewards surround themselves with constructive critical-thinking colleagues. Warren Buffett and Charlie Munger have thrived by sharing advice with one another over the years.[15] An open environment based on trust, which is also safe enough to allow for sparring and constructive conflict, allows for critical analysis of ideas and questioning of assumptions. Steward leaders surround themselves with colleagues who will openly say what they think. Critical feedback helps to mitigate against behavior biases.

Some leaders have mentors with whom they discuss their challenges. Warren Buffett and Bill Gates have a bond that has lasted many years. In the relationship, Bill Gates (who is 25 years Buffett's junior) has referred to himself as Buffett's student – a clear indication of his respect for the legendary investor. Learning from other industries can be helpful in highlighting blind spots. While many do this informally already, there may be scope for steward leaders to exchange and support one another in more formal peer coaching relationships, with leaders coaching one another across industries.

Well-stewarded organizations not only keep critical thinking at the top, but also build a culture of diversity in thinking and working at all levels. An open environment with diverse teams with different perspectives, and freedom to share these, promotes independent thoughts and better quality team outcomes.

Fighting behavior biases in an organization starts during the hiring process. Recruiting people with the same education or cultural background tends to result in groupthink. While there is a natural human preference to surround oneself with similar people, it is a dangerous path to take in terms of reinforcing behavior biases.

Great stewards encourage diversity of opinion. When people with different skills and backgrounds meet, diverse views expressed can potentially reduce behavior biases.

In the early 1990s, for example, Samsung sent international recruiting officers (IROs) abroad to bring in non-Korean MBAs and PhDs. Through improved quality of senior-level discussions, Samsung injected some highly incompatible business practices into its business model in recognition of the importance of diversity.[16]

Even with a diverse workplace, regular opportunities and invitations to challenge, to have wild ideas, are necessary. Great stewards create opportunities to discuss out-of-the-box ideas with people reporting to them. While this does not imply that all ideas should be acted upon, often wild ideas can serve as the kernel to build upon for another idea. Great innovations are often the combinations of elements of different ideas.

Leadership Transition Risk

Successful transition is necessary if stewardship is to carry on from one generation to the next. Failed leadership transition is therefore a major threat to stewardship. No matter what industry a business operates in, where it is located, or its form of ownership, leadership transition happens over time. Great stewards who have built or expanded a successful business eventually need to pass the business on to the next generation. "Choosing a successor is the most important business decision you will ever make," observed GE's Jack Welch.[17]

Leadership transition refers not only to the inter-generational transition within family businesses, but also C-suite level transition. Transition from one leader to the next is a continuous process to be cautiously managed to ensure excellence in leadership over the long term.

Leadership transition is crucial to continuity. But it is a process that is prone to risk – the risk of negligence, retirees staying on too long, choosing the wrong person, losing strong internal candidates to competitors, and outgoing leaders taking away their skills and networks. The process requires a thorough understanding of people and their psychology.

The stakes are high. For companies that manage leadership transition badly, the result is the same in the end: the business collapses miserably. This may sound far-fetched. But it happens.

Consider the story of Dr An Wang (1920–1990), a Chinese-American inventor who made an important contribution to the development of magnetic core memory. In 1951, Wang founded Wang Laboratories, and the company grew an average of 40 percent a year for the next 33 years. In 1986, Wang Laboratories was a $3 billion enterprise employing 30,000 people. Wang gave generously to education and charity and was known as one of Boston's greatest philanthropists.

In the 1980s, Wang made two decisions that proved to be mistakes. First, the company concentrated on word processors and minicomputers, not personal computers. Wang Laboratories' profits fell when the PC revolution started. Second, he chose his son Frederick Wang as the company's president in late 1986.

Charles Kenney described the leadership transition in *Riding the Runaway Horse*: "Wang was determined to pass his personal control of his company to his older son in keeping with Chinese tradition. He groomed Frederick for this from the time he was 26 and ignored the evidence that his son was not equal to the tasks he was assigned. Wang Laboratories' serious problems started with Frederick's move to the top. When directors objected, pointing out he had made a botch of his last job (product development), the doctor replied, 'He is my son.'"[18]

After the firm reported a $424 million loss in 1989, An Wang fired his son, a year before his own death from cancer. Wang Laboratories filed for bankruptcy protection on August 18, 1992. As part of the bankruptcy process, the company's headquarters, Wang Towers, was sold at auction. The complex, which originally cost $60 million to build, was sold in 1994 for $525,000. After renovation, it was subsequently sold in 1998 for over $100 million.

Another example is how Dow Jones failed to survive into the sixth generation of family control. The Bancroft family had owned Dow Jones since 1902 and controlled it as a publicly traded company since 1963. When, in 2007, Rupert Murdoch offered shareholders $5 billion to acquire the company, the family in-fighting started and the sale to Murdoch in 2011 was contentious. Family members questioned Murdoch's journalistic practices and they viewed leadership transition at Dow Jones as a failure. As one family member wrote, "We did a deal with the devil and it really saddens me [that] the editorial of this quasi-public trust that has been on the vanguard of world journalism for years is not in good hands. That I am really struggling with."

To plan for the future, great stewards decide on what the future might be, how the business should be led going forward, and what characteristics and skills are needed for the leadership role. Successful leadership transition requires long-term vision and planning.

With long-term vision and succession planning, Estée Lauder ensures continuity and growth in a family business. Estée Lauder and her husband Joseph Lauder founded the Estée Lauder Company in 1946. The company quickly expanded sales from New York City to other cities in the US. In 1960, the company started expanding internationally.

The family developed business leaders within the family. Leonard, Estée and Joseph's oldest son, joined the family business in 1958 and was groomed for leadership early in his tenure. He was charged with the responsibility of taking care of one of the key stakeholders – the buyers. In 1972, he became president, and then was named CEO and chairman.

From 1973, Estée Lauder reduced her role in the company's day-to-day operations but stayed on as the chairman of the company board. In 1995, she stepped away completely, assuming the honorary title of founding chair. Leonard became chair of the board and was chief executive until 1999.

Leonard Lauder's son, William Lauder, joined the family business in 1986 as a regional marketing director. To gain leadership experience, William Lauder took various positions requiring steadily larger responsibility. In 2004, William Lauder was named CEO of the family business. He became executive chairman in July 2009, while his father became the chairman emeritus.

Leonard Lauder summarized the philosophy behind the company's success: "We think in decades. Our competitors think in quarters." This long-term vision and succession planning has indeed served the leadership transition well.

Leadership Feuding Risk

Family businesses bring with them the risk of sibling feuds, parent–child conflict, and family in-fighting of various forms. There are numerous negative factors causing family wars: money, ego, power, nepotism, negative opinion, poor performance, lack of respect, lack of vision, to list a few.

From India to the US, magazines and newspapers are full of examples of business families battling over the control and fortune of the family. Family in-fighting has tarnished the reputation of many large businesses, even those considered among the best-run companies in the world. With blood ties, family conflicts are more damaging than normal corporate power struggles. They can destroy once well-stewarded businesses.

Of course, family businesses do not have a monopoly on feuds. Corporate power struggles are common. Executives with self-serving motives can maximize their own goals and interests at the expense of the company's. They might overpower others, disregard the perspectives and feelings of colleagues, undermine teammates, and lash out at colleagues who they consider to be a threat to their job. In their narrow minds, position and power are on their top list, not stewardship. Power struggles cripple companies.

At the very top of the organization, leadership feuding can be even more damaging where there are dual leaders or co-CEOs. Disagreements between leading duos are commonplace and destructive. Martha Stewart Living Omnimedia introduced a co-CEO structure in July 2008. The company explained the strategy as "one plus one equals three." It lost $15.7 million in the year – leading to the outright departure of one CEO. "There was tension," the company's chairman admitted.[19]

The acrimony that unfolded among the three Kwok brothers heading Sun Hung Kai Properties, one of Hong Kong's most successful conglomerates, filled tabloid pages across Asia for years on end. Amid the feud, one of the brothers received a jail sentence for colluding with the government. In 2012, the news of the arrest of two of the brothers by the anti-corruption agency wiped $4.9 billion from the company's market value.

Or consider the case of Guccio Gucci (1881–1953), the founder of Gucci. Once a liftboy at the Savoy Hotel in London, Guccio Gucci was impressed with the elegant travel bags he carried. In 1906, he started making travel bags in Florence. In 1938, Gucci expanded his business to Rome and, later, his sons joined the company. In 1953, Gucci opened its Manhattan store. The sons, Aldo and Rodolfo, went on to take over the company and improved the family business exponentially.

In 1977, Aldo made his son Paolo Gucci vice-president and managing director of Gucci Shops and Gucci Perfumes of America. As chief designer, Paolo Gucci claimed to design 80 percent of the Gucci items. However, only one year later, Paolo Gucci was fired by his uncle Rodolfo. According to Paolo, he fell out with his uncle as the family wanted to keep the company's somewhat old-fashioned ways.

In 1982, the family feuds escalated with suits initiated by Paolo Gucci against his father, his brothers, and his cousin for compensation of $13 million. The defendants filed countersuits, in part to prevent Paolo Gucci from producing competitive leather goods with the family name. Paolo then provided documents against his father for tax evasion. In 1986, Aldo Gucci, the 81-year-old father, was imprisoned for over a year for evading $7 million in taxes.

Financial scandals and family in-fighting considerably damaged the company's reputation. Split by the bitter family dispute, Gucci sold the family business in 1988. Paolo Gucci received around $41 million for his share in the business. In 1993, claiming debts of $90 million, Paolo Gucci declared bankruptcy. He died two years later aged 64.

Companies and leaders can manage the risk of leadership feuding by enlisting the right people, sharing power, defining roles, respecting others, and resolving conflicts.

Building a united leadership team takes time, focus, and energy. It takes time to enlist the right people – stewards, team members who care more about the well-being of the organization. Mutual trust, respect, and clear responsibility and roles are indispensable for a leadership team to work. Mutual respect underpins trust among team members and trust makes it possible to delegate and collaborate. When people with complementary skills and clearly defined roles are willing to work together, the risk of feuding will be reduced.

Companies ought to set rules and provide training before problems surface. If a power struggle is recognized early, by following the rules, it might be fixed quickly through honest and open conversations.

Great stewards make a distinction between power and influence. Stewarding is about influence, not power; it is about using influence, resources, and time to make an impact for the social good. Agents with too much ego tend to focus on power. Those who always want to overpower others put their personal self-interest first. They are not stewards.

Political Risk

Political risk often refers to the risk of potential loss due to macroeconomic and social policies, for example, government decisions about taxes, currency, trade tariffs or barriers, investment, wage levels, labor laws, environmental regulations, and development priorities. It may also refer to non-economic factors – destructive events such as terrorism, riots, revolutions, coups, wars, insurrections, and elections. In general, macro-level political risks have similar impacts across all foreign firms in a host country whereas micro-level risks focus on sector, firm, or project-specific risk.

For a business, political risk may directly or indirectly impact a firm by increasing the cost, reducing profit, or changing the competitive landscape. However, political risk can be measured with a probability or likelihood. As a result, like other generic risk, political risk can be managed with scenario planning or insurance.

Politics deserve to be part of corporate strategy, as proposed by David Bach and David Allen.[20] Sustained competitive advantage comes from dealing with social, political, and environmental issues, so we do not just pursue business as usual. Instead, we pursue a "non-market strategy," actively lobbying the government to change laws and regulations to shape the business landscape and reduce risk. Great stewards commit effort to integrate market and non-market strategies to manage beyond the market.

For a great steward, political risk might become a live-or-die risk when taking political sides. Great stewards often lead legendary companies that dominate the production or distribution of crucial products in an economic system. Their revenues can equate to the GDPs of small nations. Great stewards and the companies under their leadership are influential powers, both economically and politically. They can affect government policies and relations with foreign nations. Because of their power and influence, taking political sides becomes a critical risk for great stewards.

Like it or not, business leaders may have to take political sides. This often entails controversial decisions, as certain decisions follow one's religion, beliefs, and values, but contradict government laws and regulations, or vice versa. However, if taking the wrong side could mean the demise of a great company, then this risk cannot be ignored or underestimated.

Through their quality connections to a broad range of both internal and external stakeholders, steward leaders engage in a continuous cycle of scanning, checking, and seeking evidence from a broad range of sources to challenge their own thinking and assumptions. By engaging in conversations with customers, suppliers, employees, investors, NGOs, and other members of society – and listening to their responses – they continuously seek insights in order to develop sensitivity to potential vulnerabilities and pitfalls for their organizations. They check their own beliefs and biases, seeking genuine feedback and input by fostering a learning environment conducive to honest exchange. Conscious of the group dynamics at play in their leadership team, they anticipate potentially destructive conflicts early on and address these before it is too late. Additionally, they stay in touch with geopolitical developments, reflecting upon the potential impact of seemingly disconnected events. Finally, steward leaders actively think about the good of the organization – beyond their tenure – to plan their own succession in a timely and deliberate manner, thus securing their legacy for the future.

PART IV

LOOKING FORWARD

CHAPTER

Fostering Stewardship

Business continues to be the primary driver of the world's wealth generation. It is fundamental to the material improvement of human beings' lives, and therefore to the well-being of the societies in which it operates.

In a highly interconnected global economy, with increasingly complex and cross-boundary ownership structures, stewardship failures have real consequences – with shocks no longer contained within one context. In this concluding chapter, we examine the different forces at work that pose a real threat to global prosperity.

Fostering stewardship serves to counteract these forces and build a world where owners and companies can co-create wealth responsibly.

It has Become Vital to go Beyond Governance

The risks of not going down the stewardship path are real. Clear lines of responsibility for long-term business performance have been diluted and are in danger of dissolving. We have seen leaders failing to take individual responsibility for the companies they run, whether out of negligence or intentional wrongdoing. Examples abound: from BP's Deepwater Horizon oil spill in the Gulf of Mexico through the collapse of Lehman Brothers to Satyam's falsification of its accounts.

We have witnessed inflated earnings, expenses booked as capital expenditure (WorldCom), looting by the CEO and improper share deals (Tyco), inflated corporate profits to defraud investors (Global Crossing), false transactions recorded (Parmalat), and over-stated earnings (Royal Ahold).

While corporate governance is of course important and necessary, the pressures are mounting to the point where we need to go further. It is not realistic to expect that stewardship will single-handedly resolve the ills of the corporate world, but it can help mitigate against their proliferation.

Ownership structures are ever more complex. In the United States, physical persons now hold just 40 percent of publicly listed shares, compared with 84 percent in the mid-1960s. In the United Kingdom, over the last 50 years the proportion of shares held by physical persons has declined from 54 percent of public equity to 11 percent. In Japan, physical persons held just 18 percent of all public equity by 2011.[1]

As the proportion of public equity held by physical persons declines, institutional investors hold increasing amounts of the world's wealth. In 2011, this amounted to around $84.8 trillion. There are of course differences between institutional investors. One group – which includes pension funds and investment funds (includ-ing mutual funds and insurance companies) – is sometimes referred to as "traditional." A second category of institutional investors – such as sovereign wealth funds, private equity, hedge funds and exchange-traded funds – is often called "alternative."

These different types of investors have distinct investment objec-tives, time frames, and rights and responsibilities. As such, it is difficult to characterize them as a single type of investor.

However, since institutional investors hold large blocks of shares in companies, and therefore wield a great deal of influence, they are increasingly a force to be reckoned with. Diversification is a key investment strategy to manage risk, with institutional investors hold-ing positions in a range of different asset classes.

Asset Managers are not Owners

There has been an increasing trend toward intermediation in equity investment by institutional investors. Driven by a desire for greater professionalism and efficiency, many institutional investors rely on asset management firms.

Globally, asset management firms were estimated to have about $76.4 trillion under management at the end of 2013.[2] Asset management is a concentrated industry, with the top 20 managers' share of total assets under management at 41 percent.

The danger of this is that many asset managers – since they are not owners of the companies but rather intermediaries – seek to maximize returns on their portfolios rather than to act as owners. They therefore have little incentive to hold executives of the firms they invest in accountable, and thus fail to protect the interests of their investors – the ultimate shareholders and owners.

A common practice at asset management firms is for fund managers (referred to as investment advisers in the United States) to use different investment strategies and to hold positions in many hundreds – or more – of companies. This further increases the fragmentation of holdings.

For many of these fund managers, job security is based on the performance of the fund, often on a relatively short-term basis (quarterly, semi-annually), putting an emphasis on short-term performance.[3] Pressure for performance and diversification has contributed to a shortening of holding periods. For example, in the United States in 1980, the average holding period was five years, whereas in 2009 it was less than five months.[4]

Institutional Investors are Critical on the Stewardship Path

The rise of sovereign wealth funds (SWFs) in a variety of emerging market contexts is also important to note. While there are some concerns that SWFs will become activist shareholders, using their influence to extract value from investments, whether private or political, in fact many have been rather passive to date, not exercising voting rights, for example, creating a monitoring deficit.

While executives and the board have critical roles to play in securing stewardship, we urge institutional investors to acknowledge the role they have to play in stewarding the companies in which they hold shares in order to act as responsible owners. This means retaining their investment responsibilities rather than outsourcing them, as well as engaging more deeply in the companies in which they invest – possibly limiting the number of companies in which they invest to be able to devote sufficient attention to each one.

Stewardship: Owners and Managers Building a Company's Future Together

Our notion of stewardship advocates committed co-creation between owners and managers, together engaging to build a company's future.

While some have argued that the burden of such engagement is excessive, we would counter that it is the quality of connection that needs to improve rather than the quantity. It does not necessarily imply an additional reporting burden.

Throughout this book, we have looked at leaders across a range of different contexts. Our ambition has been to gain a greater understanding of this vital topic. Is there something universal about stewardship? How does it manifest in different contexts?

In some contexts, stewardship might translate into greater focus on the quality of interaction between management, boards, owners, and shareholders. In other contexts, it might mean taking ownership and initiative to fill in institutional gaps to reinforce capabilities where they are lacking. In all cases, by acknowledging and building on the connections that do exist, stewardship helps to better build firm wealth over time, lifting societal players along with it.

By showcasing a host of examples of leaders who have successfully navigated their organizations to overcome hurdles and create wealth that is both inclusive and enduring, we hope to provide fresh inspiration for thinking about long-term and responsible wealth creation and the key enabling features.

Steward leaders are often modest, diligently working to do the best for the collective while eschewing the limelight. We endeavor to celebrate the leaders who have devoted themselves to stewardship and their exceptional leadership. Understanding what they were able to achieve, and the circumstances that they overcame in order to do so, helps us to find inspiration in the potential impact we can collectively have.

Also, by understanding theory and frameworks, we seek to provide real tools for leaders to identify development areas in order to become steward leaders – in this way building the stewardship pipeline.

We believe that stewardship can help leaders to reflect upon what it means to be a responsible leader, as well as helping them find the space and resilience to adequately consider when it is necessary to sacrifice short-term benefits for long-term gain. By staying connected and having the bandwidth to understand a range of concerns, steward leaders continue to develop and learn, empowering their people and clearly preparing succession. They are self-aware and acknowledge their weaknesses, seeking themselves to be stewarded by a group of peers to avoid being undermined by their blind spots.

How do we Foster Stewardship?

Steward leaders build organizations where employees are empowered and engaged, maximizing their creative and productive contribution to the organization while developing their own capabilities. This leads to firms that deliver innovative and creative solutions to address customer needs.

With a focus on sound governance, organizations are stewarded by boards whose members are educated, aware, and effective to fulfil their supervision mandate and guide firms to fulfill their long-term purpose.

They are equipped to recognize the signs of short-termism in business, which may show up as either a tendency to under-invest (be it in R&D, development of employees, brand, or reputation) or executives who over-expend organizational resources on successive change efforts, restructuring, or M&A activity without devoting sufficient attention to the "marathons" required to sustain operational capabilities over the longer term.

Institutional investors and shareholders cultivate an ownership mentality, communicate and engage with the company, seeking to understand and build value over the long term. Rather than simply exiting when they disagree with the firm's strategy, they engage with the management to communicate their concern.

Well-stewarded firms build strong ties and are firmly embedded in the communities around them, creating greater scope for interaction, understanding, and communication. This generates a mutual respect and a recognition by societal players (including trade unions and local communities) that business is a valuable member of the greater socio-economic ecosystem.

Stewardship offers a framework to approach the decisions that need to be made by business leaders, investors, and boards to make sure that wealth is being created over the long term, while driving social good and ensuring positive short-term economic and social impact. By offering inspiring examples from Asia and around the world, together with some clarifying concepts, we hope to inject renewed energy into the discussions around the productive role that business can take by journeying on the path of stewardship.

Appendix A: The Research

Content analysis is a class of methods used to analyze text and qualitative data in a range of disciplines, including management. The core value of content analysis is the recognition of the importance of language in human cognition. The analysis of texts, such as word frequency, is considered to be an indicator of cognitive importance.[1] To management researchers, content analysis provides a replicable methodology to access deep-rooted individual or collective structures such as beliefs, values, intentions, attitudes, and philosophies.

The method has been applied to studies of corporate social responsibility, corporate culture, and other topics that are difficult to analyze using traditional quantitative and qualitative methods.[2] In a closely related study, Jeremy Short and his colleagues used word analysis to evaluate the measure of entrepreneurial orientation in family firms, as well as to examine differences between family and non-family firms along various dimensions of an entrepreneurial orientation.[3] In this preliminary study, we apply content analysis to study stewardship using annual reports.

One of the most important communication tools available to a company is its annual report. Inevitably, companies make an effort to put their best foot forward on the pages of an annual report. Nonetheless, the report's text can be a source of crucial information about the top managers' actions, thought patterns, management philosophy, and beliefs that are related to stewardship. Importantly, published research reveals a positive relationship between organizational actions and outcomes projected in the annual reports. For example, research shows that assertions of corporate social responsibility correspond to actual behavior.[4] Similarly, the degree to which a firm asserts its innovativeness generally relates to its reputation for innovation and the numbers of trademarks applied for by the firm.[5]

Companies Potentially Ranking High or Low on Stewardship

In our research, we compared two groups of companies by creating two contrasting word lists of about 1.5 million words each using the companies' annual reports. We labeled one group as "potentially ranking high on stewardship" and the other as "potentially ranking low on stewardship." We then counted and analyzed the words they used, and their frequency of use, in their annual reports. Because we worked with two portfolios of companies rather than individual companies, the two lists of words we harvested offer characteristics that are relatively stable over a long period of time, and are unlikely to be skewed by any individual company's unique attributes or idiosyncrasies.

In nominating companies for each group, we considered the general characteristics of stewardship (e.g., responsibility, long-term view, wealth creation, social good, positive impact). For the "potentially ranking high on stewardship" companies, we looked at rankings such as the World's Most Admired Companies and the Top 20 Best Companies for Leadership; sought consensus within our team on what and who represents strong stewardship; and thought about companies that have revolutionized our way of life while leaving a positive imprint on their local community and beyond (Table A.1). That is how we arrived at 20 names including Berkshire Hathaway, Coca-Cola, Nestlé, BMW, Toyota, Singapore Airlines, Hutchison Whampoa, and Tata Consulting Services.

Negative lists are always easier to compile. To scout for companies "potentially ranking low on stewardship," all we had to do was visit existing rankings such as the worst corporate accounting scandals; largest bankruptcies in US history; and news stories of fraud, corruption, and mismanagement. In the end, we settled on using pre-downfall annual reports of 17 companies, including Lehman Brothers, Enron, Satyam, and WorldCom.

We used AntConc,[6] a corpus analysis toolkit for concordance and text analysis, for our Word Content Analysis. To avoid splitting hairs and to ensure that our effort would concentrate on words for which frequency and usage were significant, we drew up a set of rules and cut-off points. For example, a word was only considered distinct if it appeared in the sample more than 20 times; the difference between its incidence in one group as opposed to the other group was likewise more than 20 occurrences; lastly, this difference had to be greater

Table A.1   Companies selected as potentially ranking high and low on stewardship

Companies potentially ranking high on stewardship	Companies potentially ranking low on stewardship
BASF	Adelphia Communications
Berkshire Hathaway	CAO
BMW	Comcast
Coca-Cola	Diamond Foods
Daimler	Enron
General Electric	HealthSouth
Google	Hollinger
Hutchison Whampoa	Lehman Brothers
IBM	Nortel
Microsoft	Olympus
Nestlé	Penn West
Procter & Gamble	Qwest Communications
Samsung	Refco
Siemens	Satyam
Singapore Airlines	Sino-Forest Corporation
Tata Consulting Services	Tyco
Telefonica	WorldCom
Temasek	
Toyota	
Unilever	

than 20 percent of the word's total count (across both groups). These criteria could be described as a "20/20/20" rule.

For example, the word "alleged" appeared 107 times in the sample of companies potentially ranking low on stewardship, and 36 times in the sample of companies potentially ranking high on stewardship. It was considered distinct to the companies potentially ranking low on stewardship as 107 > 20, (107-36) > 20 and (107-36) / (107 + 36) > 20 percent.

Subsequently, data cleaning removed words like proper names (of persons, cities, currency units, etc.), words with similar meanings and words derived from the same root. In this way, non-recurring words and words that showed up in equal counts in annual reports from both groups of companies were eliminated. As a result, the words that came out of this exercise were not only distinct but also specific to either companies potentially ranking low on stewardship or potentially ranking high on stewardship. In all, the exercise yielded 1252 "positive" words as compared with 758 "negative" words.[7]

Stewardship Words: Key Dimensions

As a next step, we classified these words along a discrete set of dimensions, including:

- Orientation: Time, extreme emotion, tone (positive, negative, neutral)
- Stakeholders: Employees, customers, other stakeholders
- Leadership: Personal references, beliefs/values/philosophy,
- governance
- Business: Financial, strategy, risk.

How did the language we found in annual reports differ between companies potentially ranking high and low on stewardship? Let us have a look at each of the above dimensions.

Orientation comparison

Time   We found that companies potentially ranking high on stewardship tended to use words such as *long-term, continually, continuously, years,* and *decades.* In contrast, companies potentially ranking low on stewardship used words like *daily, days, months,* and *presently.* The number of words they used in reference to continuity was relatively insignificant.

Extreme emotion   Companies potentially ranking high on stewardship tended to use emphatic words such as *absolute, always, completely, ever, never, everything, perfect, precious.* They used the word *yes* more frequently than other companies.

Companies potentially ranking low on stewardship used extreme words to describe customer complaints (e.g., in their assessment, customers *abuse* return policies, insurance coverage terms), financial performance (*extraordinary, super*). They used the word *no* more frequently than companies potentially ranking high on stewardship. This is consistent with previous research that deceiving CEOs used more words conveying extreme positive emotion, and extreme negative words to shift blame to others.[8]

Tone   Companies potentially ranking high on stewardship tended to use words with a positive tone, such as *boost, achieve.* The upbeat tone is consistent with other research into the general bias toward positive language in annual reports. Companies potentially ranking low on stewardship tended to use more neutral and negative words, such as *moved, obtained*. This was particularly telling when the "downcast" tone clashed with words that express extremely positive emotion (*extraordinary, super*).

Stakeholder comparison

Employees   Describing their relationship with employees, companies potentially ranking high on stewardship used words such as *aligned, bonuses, career, colleagues, compensation, diversity, employees, encourage, entitlement, grooming,* and *recognition*. Such words seem more oriented toward ongoing relationships with employees and their development. Companies potentially ranking low on stewardship used words such as *appraisal, assigned, dismissed, evaluated, hire, job, nonqualified, payroll, replaced, replacement, uncommitted, unemployment,* and *wage*. This is reflective of agency-theory thinking where management evaluates employees and monitors employees tightly.

Customers   Companies potentially ranking high on stewardship used words like *lifecycle, user, consumers, client, warranty, product, reliable, products,* and *quality* to a greater degree. Companies potentially ranking low on stewardship often used words like *complaint, allege (alleging, alleges, alleged, allegedly), purchaser/purchasers*. Companies potentially ranking high on stewardship describe customers with words like *user, consumers, client*; companies potentially ranking low on stewardship referred to customers as *purchasers*. Arguably, the underlying picture is one where companies potentially ranking high on stewardship focus on enhancing customer value whereas companies potentially ranking low on stewardship are dealing with complaints from customers. Nevertheless, they downplayed or rationalized customer complaints through words such as *alleging* – an approach unlikely to engage customers in the long run.

Other stakeholders   Companies potentially ranking high on stewardship used a wide range of words to describe their relationships with other stakeholders – words including *academic, air, anti, carbon, child, children, climate, collaboration, communities, cooperation, CSR, culture, dialog, dialogue, ecological, economical, environment, families, science, stakeholder, transparency,* and *well-being.* This mirrors their long-term approach to building rapport with local communities and the broader society. By comparison, companies potentially ranking low on stewardship used words like *appeal, arbitration, attorney, attorneys, civil, claims, court, covenants, criticized, defendant, defendants, delinquencies, delinquency, denied, discharged, enforceability, jurisdiction, lawsuit, lawsuits, legislative, litigation, petition, petitions, plaintiff, punitive, rulings, settlement, settlements, suit,* and *theft.*

Leadership comparison

Personal pronouns and references   Texts generated by companies potentially ranking high on stewardship often contained personal pronouns, such as *her, me, mine, my, our, ourselves, personnel, she, their, them, themselves, they, we, you, your.* In contrast, companies potentially ranking low on stewardship generally avoided using such words.

Beliefs, values, philosophy   Companies potentially ranking high on stewardship tended to use proactive and positive words such as *appropriateness, balanced, capabilities, challenge, concept, confidence, contribute, deed, fulfilled, heart, help, helps, hope, leads, learning, led, responsibility, responsible, role, shared, steward, stewardship, sustainability, true,* and *vision.* This would seem to indicate an emphasis on a larger social good.

Companies potentially ranking low on stewardship tend to use reactive and neutral words to describe management beliefs.

Governance   When describing their auditing practices, companies potentially ranking high on stewardship use words such as *audit, audited, auditing, auditor, audits, Deloitte, PWC.* In contract, *unaudited* is the only word standing out when companies potentially ranking low on stewardship describe their auditing practices.

Business comparison

Financial   When describing their financial situation, companies potentially ranking high on stewardship typically used general accounting words such as *baseline, budget, buyback, capex, capped, cash flow, ceiling, EBIT, hurdle, margin, overheads, profit, profitable, profit, refinancing, reinvested, revenue, share,* and *share price.*

By contrast, companies potentially ranking low on stewardship tended to use more words related to debt. These included *bankruptcy, borrowed, charge, charged, debt, defaults, downgrade, due, fines, leverage, liable, loan, loss, modified, obligations, option, options, revision,* and *revisions.* In combinations, these words gave an impression of risky leverage, high financing cost, and high bankruptcy probability. Companies potentially ranking low on stewardship also gave more attention to *option* as related to the structure of management compensation. In some instances, the larger the extent to which managers are compensated through options, the higher the likelihood that they will manipulate stock prices in order to increase the options' value.

Strategy Companies potentially ranking high on stewardship often used words like *advertising, brand, brands,* and *trademark.* They also used words related to innovation, e.g., *center, centers, create, develop, ideas, initiatives, innovate, patent, pioneering, R&D, research, revolution, scientific, technologies, transformation, trends,* and *ventures.* In contrast, companies potentially ranking low on stewardship use words such as *agreements, alliances, contractually, mergers, outsourcing, transaction, transfers,* etc. to describe their approach.

Risk Words such as *aware, assesses, hedging, preparation, prepared, prevention,* and *prudential* are used by potentially well-stewarded companies to describe their risk management mechanisms. When companies potentially ranking low on stewardship manage risk, they often use words like *mitigate* and *mitigation.* The words starting with "un-" favored by companies potentially ranking low on stewardship include *unobservable, unrealized,* and *unspecified,* which is yet another sign of uncertainty in their risk management practices.

Toward an Implied Stewardship Score

The Word Content Analysis we outlined above allows us to distil some key characteristics shared by companies potentially ranking high on stewardship. However, comparing and contrasting words may not give us the whole picture.

To further study the robustness and significance of stewardship characteristics, we compared certain aspects of companies potentially ranking high on stewardship with those of companies potentially ranking low on stewardship using univariate analysis.

The degree of stewardship as reflected in annual reports was defined in an implied stewardship score, which was calculated using the difference between the positive and negative word counts relative to the overall combined positive and negative word counts.

This formula allows for comparisons across companies as each company is unique when publishing their annual reports. Some companies provide minimal amounts of information with only a few pages in the annual reports. Other companies provide significant amounts of information. For example, Delek Group Limited produced a 722-page annual report in 2013.

Our empirical study is based on global companies with USD sales above $10 billion in 2013. The sales data was collected from Thomson One, and more than 1000 active global companies met the sales threshold. We collected the annual reports for the past three years from company websites. Some annual reports were protected with passwords, or in local languages, or too short, or not available. In total, we calculated the implied stewardship score for 234 companies that issued 10-K wrap reports (summary reports) and 638 companies that issued traditional annual reports (Figure A.1).[9]

Certain companies might attempt to manage public impressions and mitigate negative exposure by using a biased language. Due to the relative bias toward positive language in traditional annual reports,

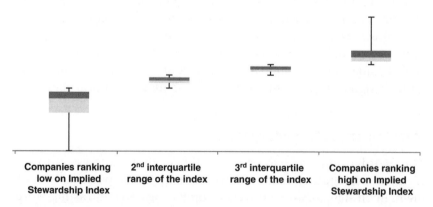

| Companies ranking low on Implied Stewardship Index | 2nd interquartile range of the index | 3rd interquartile range of the index | Companies ranking high on Implied Stewardship Index |

Figure A.1   Implied stewardship score 10-K wrap report

implied stewardship scores from traditional annual reports are less reliable for further studies.

By contrast, the 10-K wrap is the 10-K filed with the SEC along with some additional editorial from the company. Companies are therefore less likely to violate the basic premise of financial reporting, and the information contained is consistent with actual firm performance in stewardship. Therefore, we conducted a pilot study with an implied stewardship score of 234 companies (i.e., Implied Stewardship Index) that issued 10-K reports.

What Does the Implied Stewardship Score Tell us?

The implied stewardship score distribution is not symmetric around zero. In other words, companies with more negative than positive words receive a negative score, but their score does not drop significantly below zero. The asymmetric distribution brings no impact on the mean tests when we form the four groups into quartiles.

We divided the 234 companies into four groups:

- Companies ranking low on our Implied Stewardship Index, implied stewardship score 0.091 and below, 58 companies;
- 2nd interquartile range of the index, implied stewardship score 0.0934 to 0.1871, 59 companies;
- 3rd interquartile range of the index, implied stewardship score 0.1878 to 0.2632, 58 companies;
- Companies ranking high on our Implied Stewardship Index, implied stewardship score 0.2660 and above, 59 companies.

With data from Worldscope, we compared specific measures of the bottom group with those of the top group, and left out all other companies in the middle. In this way we could test how companies ranking high on our Implied Stewardship Index behaved differently from companies ranking low on our Implied Stewardship Index.

Are companies ranking high on our Implied Stewardship Index less likely to engage in large-scale downsizing? We collected employee data for the years 2007, 2008, 2009, and 2010. Employees represented the number of both full- and part-time employees of the company. We then calculated the percentage change year over year. From the three percentages, we chose the lowest percentage indicating large-scale downsizing during the 2008–2010 economic crisis.

Table A.2   Large-scale downsizing t-test – Two-sample assuming unequal variances

	Bottom	Top
Mean	−0.09085	−0.04136
Variance	0.029566	0.005261
Observations	57	54
Hypothesized Mean Difference	0	
df	76	
t Stat	−1.9937	
P(T<=t) one-tail	0.024886	
t Critical one-tail	1.665151	
P(T<=t) two-tail	0.049773	
t Critical two-tail	1.991673	

T-test results (Table A.2) indicate that there is a significant difference between companies ranking low on our Implied Stewardship Index and companies ranking high on our Implied Stewardship Index (−9 percent vs. −4 percent, p < 0.05) (Figure A.2). During the worst years of the last crisis, companies ranking low on our Implied Stewardship Index cut on average 9 percent of their workforce; while companies ranking high on our Implied Stewardship Index cut on average 4 percent.

Do companies ranking high on our Implied Stewardship Index use less debt?   T-test results (Table A.3) indicate that there is a significant difference between companies ranking low on our Implied Stewardship Index and companies ranking high on our Implied Stewardship Index

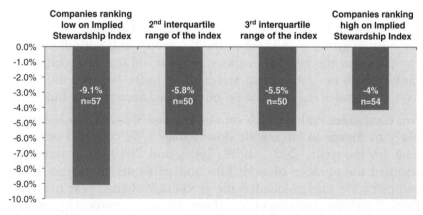

Figure A.2   Large-scale downsizing by companies ranking low to high on Implied Stewardship Index

Table A.3   Total debt as percentage of total assets 5-year average t-test – Two-sample assuming unequal variances

	Bottom	Top
Mean	29.79015	20.51589
Variance	575.7462	158.8587
Observations	56	59
Hypothesized Mean Difference	0	
df	82	
t Stat	2.574824	
P(T<=t) one-tail	0.005913	
t Critical one-tail	1.663649	
P(T<=t) two-tail	0.011826	
t Critical two-tail	1.989319	

(29.8 vs. 20.5, p < 0.01) (Figure A.3). With a total debt to total assets ratio of 29.8 percent, companies ranking low on our Implied Stewardship Index were more leveraged; while companies ranking high on our Implied Stewardship Index were less leveraged with 20.5 percent total debt to total assets.

Do companies ranking high on our Implied Stewardship Index have a higher liquidity?   T-test results (Table A.4) indicate that there is a significant difference between companies ranking low on our Implied Stewardship Index and companies ranking high on our Implied Stewardship Index (0.87 vs. 1.14, p < 0.05) (Figure A.4). Generally, the quick ratio[10] should be 1:1 or higher. However, companies ranking

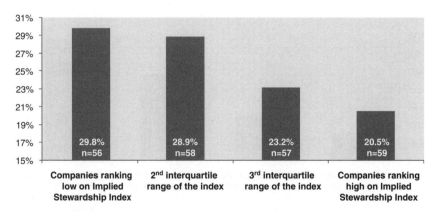

Figure A.3   Total debt as percentage of total assets, 5-year average by companies ranking low to high on Implied Stewardship Index

Table A.4   Quick ratio, 5-year average, t-test – Two-sample assuming unequal variance

	Bottom	Top
Mean	0.874206	1.143152
Variance	0.184956	0.707724
Observations	33	57
Hypothesized Mean Difference	0	
df	87	
t Stat	−2.00344	
P(T<=t) one-tail	0.024121	
t Critical one-tail	1.662557	
P(T<=t) two-tail	0.048242	
t Critical two-tail	1.987608	

low on our Implied Stewardship Index have a quick ratio of less than 1; while companies ranking high on our Implied Stewardship Index have a quick ratio higher than 1. The higher the ratio, the better the capability to meet current obligations using liquid assets.

Do companies ranking high on our Implied Stewardship Index have a higher ROE?[11]   T-test results (Table A.5) indicate that there is a significant difference between companies ranking low on our Implied Stewardship Index and companies ranking high on our Implied Stewardship Index (10 vs. 24.9, p < 0.01) (Figure A.5). Over the last five years, companies ranking low on our Implied Stewardship Index generated on average 10 percent return on equity per share; while companies ranking high on our Implied Stewardship Index

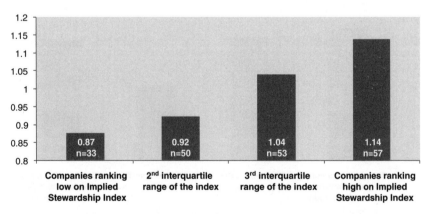

Figure A.4   Liquidity measured by quick ratio, 5-year average by companies ranking low to high on Implied Stewardship Index

Table A.5   Return on equity per share, 5-year average, t-test – Two-sample assuming unequal variance

	Bottom	Top
Mean	10.09499	24.88341
Variance	246.7145	943.6332
Observations	47	51
Hypothesized Mean Difference	0	
df	76	
t Stat	−3.0344	
P(T<=t) one-tail	0.001649	
t Critical one-tail	1.665151	
P(T<=t) two-tail	0.003298	
t Critical two-tail	1.991673	

generated over 24.9 percent return on equity per share on average. The difference of about 15 percent per year is significant statistically.

Do companies ranking high on our Implied Stewardship Index have higher stock returns (including dividends)?   T-test results (Table A.6) indicate that there is a significant difference between companies ranking low on our Implied Stewardship Index and companies ranking high on our Implied Stewardship Index (17.5 vs. 27.4, p < 0.01) (Figure A.6). Over the last five years, companies ranking low on our Implied Stewardship Index generated on average 17.5 percent stock returns annually; while companies ranking high on our Implied Stewardship Index generated over 27.4 percent stock returns annually on

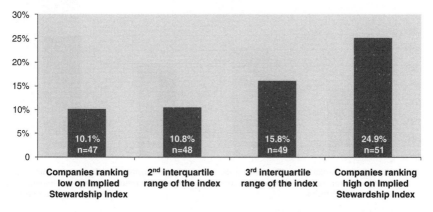

Figure A.5   Return on equity per share, 5-year average by companies ranking low to high on Implied Stewardship Index

Table A.6   Stock returns (including dividends), 5-year return, t-test – Two-sample assuming unequal variances

	Bottom	Top
Mean	17.49203	27.39528
Variance	229.5082	623.3045
Observations	54	56
Hypothesized Mean Difference	0	
df	91	
t Stat	−2.52517	
P(T<=t) one-tail	0.006647	
t Critical one-tail	1.661771	
P(T<=t) two-tail	0.013295	
t Critical two-tail	1.986377	

average. The difference of about 10 percent annually is statistically significant.

Do companies ranking high on our Implied Stewardship Index exhibit less stock volatility?   Price volatility = measure of a stock's average annual price movement to a high and low from a mean price for each year. For example, a stock's price volatility of 20 percent indicates that the stock's annual high and low price has shown a historical variation of +20 percent to −20 percent from its annual average price.

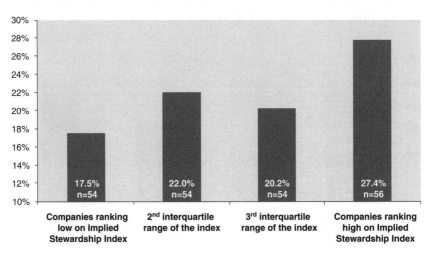

Figure A.6   Stock return (including dividends), 5-year average by companies ranking low to high on Implied Stewardship Index

Table A.7   Price volatility, t-test – Two-sample assuming unequal variances

	Bottom	Top
Mean	28.11765	22.94585
Variance	112.8663	3.88543
Observations	48	53
Hypothesized Mean Difference	0	
df	87	
t Stat	2.742297	
P(T<=t) one-tail	0.003703	
t Critical one-tail	1.662557	
P(T<=t) two-tail	0.007406	
t Critical two-tail	1.987608	

T-test results (Table A.7) indicate that there is a significant difference between companies ranking low on our Implied Stewardship Index and companies ranking high on our Implied Stewardship Index (28.1 vs. 22.9, p < 0.01) (Figure A.7). Companies ranking low on our Implied Stewardship Index showed a historical variation of 28 percent from average; while companies ranking high on our Implied Stewardship Index showed about 22.9 percent price volatility. The difference is statistically significant.

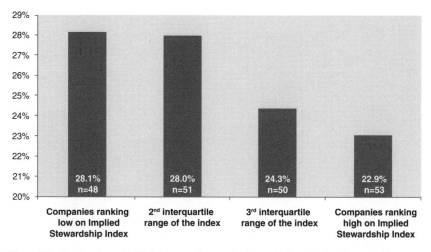

Figure A.7   Stock price volatility by companies ranking low to high on Implied Stewardship Index

References

Introduction

1. Merriam-Webster's Collegiate Dictionary, 2005.
2. Rosenzweig, P. (2007). *The Halo Effect*. New York, NY: Free Press.
3. All figures quoted throughout are in US dollars unless otherwise stated.
4. Mizik, N. and Jacobson, R. (2003). Trading off between value creation and value appropriation: the financial implications of shifts in strategic emphasis. *Journal of Marketing*, 67(1): 63–76.

Chapter 1

1. Lala, R. M. (2004). *The Creation of Wealth: The Tatas from the 19th to the 21st Century*. New Delhi: Penguin Books India.
2. Pultarova, T. (2014). End of the Ambassador – India's iconic car. *Engineering and Technology Magazine*. http://eandt.theiet.org/news/2014/may/ambassador-production.cfm.
3. Ratan Tata's Legacy. *The Economist* (December 2012).
4. Ibid.
5. Ibid.
6. Singhal, M., Meteoric rise. *Business Today* (March 16, 2014).
7. Frost & Sullivan (2014). Chairman Emeritus, Tata Sons, Mr. Ratan Tata receives the Frost & Sullivan Growth, Innovation and Leadership Award for Visionary Innovation at GIL India: 2014 [Press release]. Retrieved from http://www.prnewswire.com/news-releases/chairman-emeritus-tata-sons-mr-ratan-tata-receives-the-frost–sullivan-growth-innovation-and-leadership-award-for-visionary-innovation-at-gil-india-2014-277050831.html.
8. Engardio, P., The last Rajah. *BusinessWeek* (August 2, 2007).
9. Ahmed, R. and Chowdhury, A. Tata Sons appoints successor. *The Wall Street Journal* (November 24, 2011). Retrieved from http://www.wsj.com/articles/SB10001424052970204630904577055883710911036.
10. Hill, A., Tata can take a long view on succession. *Financial Times* (November 28, 2011). Retrieved from http://www.ft.com/intl/cms/s/0/a04030ce-1762-11e1-b00e-00144feabdc0.html#axzz3TdXAorTA.
11. Mærsk. (2015). Mærsk Major Shareholders: Shareholders with more than 5% of share capital or votes. Retrieved April 28, 2015, from http://investor.maersk.com/ownership-profile.cfm.

12. Wienberg, C. and Schwartzkopff, F., McKinney Moeller, Denmark's richest man, dies at 98. *Bloomberg Business* (April 16, 2012).
13. Adeney, M., Mærsk Mc-Kinney Møller obituary: Magnate who built the world's greatest shipping empire and Denmark's biggest corporation, AP Møller-Mærsk group, Obituary. *The Guardian* (April 22, 2012). Retrieved from http://www.theguardian.com/world/2012/apr/22/maersk-mckinney-moller-obituary.
14. Von Haffner, C. D. (2014). The values are constant in a complex world.
15. Mærsk (2015) *Mærsk Group Core Values.* www.maersk.com/en/the-maersk-group/about-us/maersk-group-core-values.
16. Lakhani, A. (2013). *7 Lessons for Effective B2B Content Marketing via the Mærsk Line Case Study.* Retrieved from http://www.searchdecoder.com/b2b-content-marketing.
17. Berrill, P. (2014). Mærsk values: Everything is relative. Retrieved December 4, 2014, from http://www.tradewindsnews.com/TWplus/349930/Maersk-values-Everything-is-relative.
18. Fischer, B., Lago, U., and Liu, F. (2013). *Reinventing Giants: How Chinese Global Competitor Haier has Changed the Way Big Companies Transform.* San Francisco: Jossey-Bass.
19. Zhang, R. (2007). Raising Haier. *Harvard Business Review*, 85(2): 141–146.
20. Ibid.
21. Liker, J. K. (2004). *The Toyota Way: 14 Management Principles from the World's Greatest Manufacturer.* New York: McGraw-Hill.
22. Miller, J. (2013). The man who saved kaizen. Retrieved from http://www.gembapantarei.com/2013/09/the_man_who_saved_kaizen.html.
23. Ibid.
24. Ikujiro, N. and Hirotaka, T. (2011). The wise leader. *Harvard Business Review*, 89(5): 58–67.
25. IMD (2008). IMD Warren Buffett active in the market. Retrieved from http://www.imd.org/news/Warren-Buffett-active-in-the-market.cfm
26. IMD (2008). Warren Buffett and Eitan Wertheimer celebrate 20 years of family business research and education at IMD [press release]. Retrieved from http://www.imd.org/about/pressroom/pressreleases/Warren-Buffett-and-Eitan-Wertheimer-celebrate-20-years-of-family-business-research-and-education-at-IMD.cfm.
27. IMD (2008). Warren Buffett active in the market. Retrieved from http://www.imd.org/news/Warren-Buffett-active-in-the-market.cfm.
28. Cunningham, L. (2014). Berkshire Hathaway's Citizenship: Culture, scale and the future. Retrieved from http://www.triplepundit.com/2014/12/berkshire-hathaways-citizenship-culture-scale-future.
29. Buhayar, N. and Polson, J., Buffett Ready to Double $15 Billion Solar, Wind Bet. *Bloomberg Business* (June 10, 2014). Retrieved from http://www.bloomberg.com/news/articles/2014-06-10/buffett-ready-to-double-15-billion-solar-wind-bet.
30. Deng never held a formal title as head of state, head of the executive, or head of the Communist Party.

31. Mirsky, J., How Deng did it. *The New York Times* (October 21, 2011). Retrieved from   http://www.nytimes.com/2011/10/23/books/review/deng-xiaoping-and-the-transformation-of-china-by-ezra-f-vogel-book-review.html?pagewanted=all&_r=1.
32. An interview with Deng Xiaoping. *Time* (September 23, 1985).
33. This quote, attributed to Deng Xiaoping, has become part of China's folklore; as such, its precise origin is unclear.
34. Plate, T. (2013). *Conversations with Lee Kuan Yew: Citizen Singapore: How to build a nation*. Singapore: Marshall Cavendish Editions.
35. Lee, K. Y. (2000). *From Third World to First: The Singapore Story, 1965–2000*. New York, NY: Harper Collins.
36. Zakaria, F. (1994). Culture is destiny – A conversation with Lee Kuan Yew. *Foreign Affairs*, 73(2): 109.
37. IMD (2014). *World Competitiveness Yearbook*. Lausanne: IMD World Competitiveness Center.

Chapter 2

1. Deontology argues that decisions should be made considering the factors of one's duties and others' rights; this is distinct from, notably, consequentialism (teleology), which argues that the morality of an action is contingent on the action's outcome or result.
2. Alatas, S. F., Ghee, L.T., and Kuroda, K. (2003). *Asian Interfaith Dialogue: Perspectives on Religion, Education and Social Cohesion*. Singapore: Centre for Research on Islamic and Malay Affairs and the World Bank.
3. Ross, S. A. (1973). The economic theory of agency: The principal's problem. *American Economic Review*, 63(2): 134–139; Wiseman, R. M. and Gomez-Mejia, L. R. (1998). A behavioral agency model of managerial risk taking. *Academy of Management Review*, 23(1): 133–153. doi: 10.5465/AMR.1998.192967.
4. Eisenhardt, K. M. (1989). Agency theory: an assessment and review. *Academy of Management Review*, 14(1): 57–74. doi: 10.5465/AMR.1989.4279003.
5. Etzioni, A. (1975). *A Comparative Analysis of Complex Organizations*. New York: The Free Press.
6. Harvard Business School. (2004). Minoru Makihara, 75th AMP, 1977. Harvard Alumni Stories. Retrieved from https://www.alumni.hbs.edu/stories/Pages/story-bulletin.aspx?num=2014.
7. Davis, J. H., Schoorman, F. D., and Donaldson, L. (1997). Davis, Schoorman, and Donaldson reply: The distinctiveness of agency theory and stewardship theory. *The Academy of Management Review*, 22(3): 611–613.
8. Lichtenstein, D.R., Maxham, J.G., and Netemeyer, R.G. (2011). Employees who identify with the company boost financial performance. HBR Forum. Retrieved from https://hbr.org/2011/12/employees-who-identify-with-th.

9. Davis, J. H., Schoorman, F. D., and Donaldson, L. (1997). Davis, Schoorman, and Donaldson reply: The distinctiveness of agency theory and stewardship theory. *The Academy of Management Review*, 22(3): 611–613.
10. Ibid.
11. Ibid.
12. Matsushita, K. (1994). *Matsushita Konosuke (1894–1989): His Life & his Legacy: A Collection of Essays in Honor of the Centenary of his Birth*. Tokyo, Japan: PHP Institute.
13. Phoocharoon, P. (2013). Lesson from authentic leader: Konosuke Matsushita, founder of Panasonic. Paper presented at the 3rd Asia-Pacific Business Research Conference Kuala Lumpur, Malaysia. http://www.wbiworldconpro.com/uploads/malaysia-conference-2013/management/474-Palin.pdf.
14. Nestlé. (2014). Putting business back at the heart of society. 2014 Creating Shared Value Forum, October 9, 2014, http://www.nestle.com/media/newsand features/creating-shared-value-forum-2014-highlights.
15. Maersk. (2015c). *Financing Strategy*. Retrieved from http://investor.maersk.com/bonds-strategy.cfm.
16. Dou, E., Stan Shih offers clues to plan for Acer turnaround. *Wall Street Journal* (January 7, 2014). Retrieved from http://blogs.wsj.com/digits/2014/01/07/stan-shih-offers-clues-to-plan-for-acer-turnaround.
17. Noronha, C. (2007, November). In step with the nation. Retrieved from http://www.tata.com/aboutus/articlesinside/KmqN8d384OM=/TLYVr3YPkMU=.
18. Milton Friedman is credited with being the originator of this line of thought; as such, it is often referred to as the Friedman Doctrine.
19. Campbell, A. (1997). Stakeholders: the case in favour. *Long Range Planning*, 30(3): 446–449; Freeman, R. E. (1984). *Strategic Management: A Stakeholder Approach*. Boston: Pitman Publishing; Freeman, R.E., Harrison, J.S., and Wicks, A.C. (2007). *Managing for Stakeholders: Survival, Reputation, and Success*. New Haven: Yale University Press.
20. Ghoshal, S. (2005). Bad management theories are destroying good management practices. *Academy of Management Learning & Education*, 4(1): 75–91. doi: 10.5465/AMLE.2005.16132558.
21. Jordi, C. L. (2010). Rethinking the firm's mission and purpose. *European Management Review*, 7(4): 195–204. doi: 10.1057/emr.2010.11.
22. Mazutis, D., Ionescu-Somers, A. with Coughlan, S. and Sorell, M. (2015). How authentic is your corporate purpose? Burson Marsteller and IMD, http://powerofpurpose.burson-marsteller.com/wp-content/uploads/2015/04/BM_IMD _REPORT-How-Authentic-is-your-Corporate-Purpose.pdf.
23. Sonnenfeld, J. A. (2002). What makes great boards great. *Harvard Business Review*, 80(9): 106–113.
24. Maznevski, M. L., DiStefano, J. J., Gomez, C. B, Noorderhaven, N. G., and Wu, P.-C. (2002). Cultural dimensions at the individual level of analysis: the cultural orientations framework. *International Journal of Cross Cultural Management*, 2(3): 275–295.
25. Hofstede, G. (1991). *Cultures and Organizations – Software of the Mind*. New York: McGraw Hill.

26. House, R., Javidan, M., Hanges, P., and Dorfman, P. (2002). Understanding cultures and implicit leadership theories across the globe: An introduction to project GLOBE. *Journal of World Business*, 37(1): 3–10. doi: http://dx.doi.org/10.1016/S1090-9516(01)00069-4.

27. Javidan, M., Dorfman, P. W., De Luque, M. S., and House, R. J. (2006). In the eye of the beholder: Cross cultural lessons in leadership from Project GLOBE. *Academy of Management Perspectives*, 20(1): 67–90. doi: 10.5465/AMP.2006.19873410.

28. Waldman, D. A., Sully de Luque, M., Washburn, N. et al. (2006). Cultural and leadership predictors of corporate social responsibility values of top management: a GLOBE study of 15 countries. *Journal of International Business Studies*, 37(6): 823–837. doi: http://dx.doi.org/10.1057/palgrave.jibs.8400230.

29. Ibid.

30. Ibid.

31. Hall, E. T. (1976). *Beyond Culture*. New York: Anchor Books/Doubleday.

32. Trompenaars, F. and Hampden-Turner, C, (2012). *Riding the Waves of Culture: Understanding Diversity in Global Business* (3rd edn). New York: McGraw Hill.

33. Lewis, R. (1996). *When Cultures Collide: Managing Successfully Across Cultures*. Boston: Nicholas Brealey Publishing.

Chapter 3

1. Sinek, S., How great leaders inspire action. TED Talk. (September 2009) http://www.ted.com/talks/simon_sinek_how_great_leaders_inspire_action?language=en.

2. Pitts, G., Paul Polman: Rebuilding capitalism from the basics. *The Globe and Mail* (March 10, 2013). Retrieved from http://www.theglobeandmail.com/report-on-business/careers/careers-leadership/paul-polman-rebuilding-capitalism-from-the-basics/article9577971/?page=all.

3. Kenyon-Rouvinez, D., Schwass, J., Glemser, A.-C., and Králik, M. (2014). Succession Challenges for Asian Family Businesses: How to keep your value(s). IMD Tomorrow's Challenge. Retrieved from http://www.imd.org/research/challenges/TC059-14-succession-challenges-asian-family-businesses-schwass-kenyon-rouvinez.cfm.

4. Hudson, M., IMF Meeting Review – Austerity to Cost (October 19, 2014). Retrieved from http://michael-hudson.com/2014/10/imf-meeting-review-austerity-to-cost.

5. Hagstrom, R. (2015). *The Warren Buffett Way*. Chichester: Wiley. Retrieved April 28, 2015, from http://eu.wiley.com/WileyCDA/Section/id-817935.html.

6. Ferguson, T.W. and Kwok, V.W. (2006). Thoughts of Li Ka-Shing. Forbes (December 29, 2006). Retrieved from http://www.forbes.com/2006/12/29/li-ka-shing-biz-cx_tf_vk_1229qanda.html.

7. Studwell, J. (2007). *Asian Godfathers: Money and Power in Hong Kong and Southeast Asia*. New York, NY: Grove Press.

8. Quick ratio = (current assets-inventories)/current liabilities.

9. Crainer, S. and Dearlove, D. (2014). Shaping tomorrow. *Business Strategy Review*, 25(4): 8–13.
10. Stanford, 'You've got to find what you love,' Jobs says. *Stanford Report* (June 14, 2005).
11. Hudson, M., IMF Meeting Review – Austerity to Cost (October 19, 2014). Retrieved from http://michael-hudson.com/2014/10/imf-meeting-review-austerity-to-cost.
12. Baer, D., 22 Brilliant insights from Richard Branson. *Business Insider* (July 20, 2014). Retrieved from http://www.businessinsider.com/quotes-from-richard-branson-2014-7?op=1&IR=T.
13. Crainer, S. and Dearlove, D. (2014). Shaping tomorrow. *Business Strategy Review*, 25(4): 8–13.
14. Tanzo, R. (2015). Secret business strategies of Bill Gates and Jeff Bezos. Retrieved from http://history.cultural-china.com/Wise/wise151.html.
15. Colvin, G., Mark Zuckerberg – Founder and CEO, Facebook (50 World's Greatest Leaders). *Fortune* (March 26, 2015).
16. Barton, D. and Wiseman, M. (2014). Focusing capital on the long-term. *Harvard Business Review*, 92(1/2): 44–51.
17. Mohan, M. (2014). 101 "Hand-picked" Warren Buffett quotes on investing. Retrieved from http://www.minterest.org/best-warren-buffett-quotes-on-investing.
18. Ching, H. (2014). Address at Asia Business Leader's Award Dinner. Banqueting House, Whitehall, London, 27 October 2014.
19. Cultural China. (2015). General Wu Qi. Retrieved from http://history.cultural-china.com/Wise/wise151.html.
20. Carmichael, E. (2015b). Bill Gates quotes. Retrieved from http://www.evancarmichael.com/Famous-Entrepreneurs/556/Bill-Gates-Quotes.html.
21. Ibid.
22. Gates, B., Remarks of Bill Gates, Harvard Commencement 2007. *Harvard Gazette* (June 7, 2007).
23. The Giving Pledge. (2015). FAQ. Retrieved April 29, 2015, from http://givingpledge.org/faq.aspx.
24. Lewis, N., Giving Pledge signers gave big in 2013 but not much for today's needs. *The Chronicle of Philanthropy* (February 9, 2014).
25. Dale Carnegie was a business communication guru active in the early 20th century in the United States, who founded the Dale Carnegie Course in Effective Speaking and Human Relations.
26. Gallo, C., How Warren Buffett and Joel Osteen conquered their terrifying fear of public speaking. *Forbes* (May 16, 2013). Retrieved from http://www.Forbes.com/sites/carminegallo/2013/05/16/how-warren-buffett-and-joel-osteen-conquered-their-terrifying-fear-of-public-speaking.
27. Schroeder, A. (2009). *The Snowball: Warren Buffett and the Business of Life*. New York: Bantam Books.
28. Gallo, C., How Warren Buffett and Joel Osteen conquered their terrifying fear of public speaking. *Forbes* (May 16, 2013). Retrieved from http://www.Forbes.com/sites/carminegallo/2013/05/16/how-warren-buffett-and-joel-osteen-conquered-their-terrifying-fear-of-public-speaking.

Chapter 4

1. Carlopio, J. R., Andrewartha, G., and Armstrong, H. (2000). *Developing Management Skills in Australia*. Frenchs Forest, NSW: Pearson Education.
2. Ikujiro, N. and Hirotaka, T. (2011). The wise leader. *Harvard Business Review*, 89(5): 58–67.
3. Whiteley, A. M. and Whiteley, J. (2007). *Core Values and Organizational Change: Theory and Practice*. Hackensack, NJ: World Scientific.
4. Evolution. (2003). Sumantra Ghoshal: The company collector. *Evolution – The Business and Technology Magazine from SKF*.
5. Loy, D. (1988). *Nonduality: A Study in Comparative Philosophy*. New Haven: Yale University Press.
6. Tata. (2008). The quotable Jamsetji Tata. Retrieved from http://www.tata.com/aboutus/articlesinside/The-quotable-Jamsetji-Tata.
7. Lin, H.-C. and Hou, S.-T. (2010). Managerial lessons from the East: An interview with Acer's Stan Shih. *Academy of Management Perspectives*, 24: 6–16.
8. Ayala. (2004). Ayala Refreshes Corporate Brand, Press Release. Retrieved from http://www.ayala.com.ph/news/page/ayala-refreshes-corporate-brand.
9. UN Global Compact (2013). Fung Group: Communication on Progress 2012–2013. from https://www.unglobalcompact.org/system/attachments/28111/original/UNGC%20report%202012-13%20final%202..pdf?1376044106%3F.
10. Park, R.-R. and Barjot, D. (2008). Samsung, an Original and Competitive Social Model: The Role of the Founder, Lee Byung-Chull. University of Glasgow. Retrieved from http://www.gla.ac.uk/media/media_167104_en.pdf.
11. Ise, M., The Canon Style: Successful Japanese Style Management. *Japan Close-up* (June 2008).
12. Sadowsky, J. (2013). Ratan Tata: A shining example of business leadership in the third world. Retrieved from http://www.johnsadowsky.com/ratan-tata-a-shining-example-of-business-leadership-in-the-third-world.
13. Rediff, Ratan Tata's words of inspiration. *Rediff News* (August 26, 2008). Retrieved from http://m.rediff.com/money/2008/aug/26sli11.htm, URL no longer active.
14. McCormick, J., The World According to Azim Premji. *Stanford Alumni* (May–June 2006).
15. Buechel, B., Cordon, C., and Kralik, M. (2013). Indonesian Port Corporation: Entering the big league? IMD Case IMD-7-1494. Lausanne: IMD.
16. Nanum, A. (n.d.). In Asan's words. (n.d.). Retrieved from http://www.asan-nanum.org/eng/index/0502.php.
17. Hao-Chieh, L. and Sheng-Tsung, H. (2010). Managerial Lessons From the East: An Interview With Acer's Stan Shih. *Academy of Management Perspectives* 24(4): 6–16.
18. Ibid.
19. Lin, H.-C. and Hou, S.-T. (2010). Managerial lessons from the East: An interview with Acer's Stan Shih. *Academy of Management Perspectives* 24: 6–16.

20. Tan, S. K. (2008). Influence of Confucianism on Korean corporate culture. *Asian Profile*, 36(1): 9–20.
21. Fischer, B., Lago, U., and Liu, F. (2013). *Reinventing Giants: How Chinese Global Competitor Haier has Changed the Way Big Companies Transform*. San Francisco: Jossey-Bass.
22. Ibid.
23. Cossin, D., Coughlan, S., and Ong, B.H. (2015). *Stewardship: Fostering Responsible Long-Term Wealth Creation*. Lausanne and Singapore: Stewardship Asia Centre and IMD.
24. Kenyon-Rouvinez, D., Schwass, J., Glemser, A.-C., and Králik, M., Succession Challenges for Asian Family Businesses: How to keep your value(s). *IMD Tomorrow's Challenge* (August 2014). Lausanne: IMD. Retrieved from http://www.imd.org/research/challenges/TC059-14-succession-challenges-asian-family-businesses-schwass-kenyon-rouvinez.cfm.
25. Riti, M. D., JRD: The legend lives on. *Rediff* (July 27, 2004). Retrieved from http://www.rediff.com/money/2004/jul/27spec.htm.
26. Ibid.
27. Acer Group, A. (2005). Acer Corporate Environmental Report: Acer.
28. Xiaochuan, Z., People's Bank of China Governor's New Year message (January 19, 2015). Retrieved from http://www.bis.org/review/r150119d.htm.
29. Moore, M., China Construction Bank strains at the leash (August 24, 2009). Retrieved from http://www.telegraph.co.uk/finance/china-business/6068777/China-Construction-Bank-strains-at-the-leash.html.
30. Ramcharan, R. (2002). *Forging a Singaporean Statehood, 1965–1995: The Contribution of Japan*. The Hague: Kluwer Law International.

Chapter 5

1. Bligh, M. (2010). Personality theories of leadership. In J. M. Levine and M.A. Hogg (eds), *Encyclopedia of Group Processes & Intergroup Relations*. London, UK: SAGE, pp. 639–642.
2. Haslam, S. A., Reicher, S. D., and Platow, M.J. (2011). *The New Psychology of Leadership: Identity, Influence and Power*. Hove, East Sussex: Psychology Press.
3. Bligh, M. (2010). Personality theories of leadership. In J. M. Levine and M.A. Hogg (eds), *Encyclopedia of Group Processes & Intergroup Relations*. London, UK: SAGE, pp. 639–642.
4. Ibid.
5. Haslam, S. A., Reicher, S. D., and Platow, M.J. (2011). *The New Psychology of Leadership: Identity, Influence and Power*. Hove, East Sussex: Psychology Press.
6. Kohlrieser, G. IMD Professor George Kohlrieser comments on responsible leadership (January 21, 2009). Retrieved from http://www.imd.org/news/IMD-Professor-George-Kohlrieser-on-responsible-leadership.cfm.

7. Haslam, S. A., Reicher, S. D., and Platow, M.J. (2011). *The New Psychology of Leadership: Identity, Influence and Power.* Hove, East Sussex: Psychology Press.

8. Clifford, M. (1989). Death-defying pact. *Far Eastern Economic Review*, 70–76.

9. Do, J. H. Book revisits can-do spirit of pioneering entrepreneur. *The Korea Times* (February 27, 2015). Retrieved from www.koreatimes.co.kr/www/news/culture/2015/02/142_174302.html.

10. Kets de Vries, M. (2006). *The Leader on the Couch: A Clinical Approach to Changing People and Organizations.* San Francisco: Jossey-Bass.

11. Tabuchi, H., Eiji Toyoda, promoter of the Toyota Way and engineer of its growth, dies at 100. *The New York Times* (September 17, 2013). Retrieved from www.nytimes.com/2013/09/18/business/global/eiji-toyoda-promoter-of-toyota-way-dies-at-100.html?_r=1.

12. Ibid.

13. Kohlrieser, G., IMD Professor George Kohlrieser comments on responsible leadership (January 21, 2009). Retrieved from http://www.imd.org/news/IMD-Professor-George-Kohlrieser-on-responsible-leadership.cfm.

14. Clawson, J. G., DePalo, M., and Hwang, B. (2008). *Hyundai Group's Chung Ju-yung: A Profile in Leadership.* Case Study UVA-OB-0555, Darden Business Publishing, University of Virginia. Retrieved from http://ssrn.com/abstract=910415.

15. Treece, J. B., He put Toyota in the spotlight, but Eiji Toyoda fled the limelight. *Automotive News* (September 23, 2013). Retrieved from http://www.autonews.com/article/20130923/OEM02/309239962/he-put-toyota-in-the-spotlight-but-eiji-toyoda-fled-the-limelight.

16. Ikujiro, N. and Hirotaka, T. (2011). The Wise Leader. *Harvard Business Review*, 89(5): 58–67.

17. Zhang, R. (2007). Raising Haier. *Harvard Business Review*, 85(2): 141–146.

18. Stan Shih, Notes on intercultural communication. (2010). Retrieved from https://laofutze.wordpress.com/tag/stan-shih-biography.

19. Ibid.

20. Kelly, T., The outsider. *Forbes* (August 22, 2008).

21. CNN (2007). Transcript: Masamoto Yashiro, former chairman & CEO, Shinsei Bank. In A. Stevens (ed.): CNN. Retrieved from http://edition.cnn.com/2007/BUSINESS/01/14/boardroom.yashiro.

22. Weinberg, N., Setting sun. *Forbes* (April 20, 1998).

23. Larson, A. P. (2001). Japan's changing FDI and corporate environment. Retrieved from http://2001-2009.state.gov/p/eap/rls/rpt/4049.htm.

24. Kelly, T., The outsider. *Forbes* (August 22, 2008).

25. CNN (2007). Transcript: Masamoto Yashiro, former chairman & CEO, Shinsei Bank. In A. Stevens (ed.): CNN. Retrieved from http://edition.cnn.com/2007/BUSINESS/01/14/boardroom.yashiro.

26. Bloomberg, Online Extra: Q&A with Shinsei Bank's Masamoto Yashiro (July 1, 2001). Retrieved from http://www.bloomberg.com/bw/stories/2001-07-01/online-extra-q-and-a-with-shinsei-banks-masamoto-yashiro.

27. CNN (2007). Transcript: Masamoto Yashiro, former chairman & CEO, Shinsei Bank. In A. Stevens (ed.): CNN. Retrieved from http://edition.cnn.com/2007/BUSINESS/01/14/boardroom.yashiro.
28. Green, T., Words from Madiba: 14 of Nelson Mandela's best quotes. *International Business Times* (2013). Retrieved from http://www.ibtimes.com/words-madiba-14-nelson-mandelas-best-quotes-1497954.
29. Wilber, K. (1981). *No Boundary: Eastern and Western approaches to personal growth*. Boulder, CO: Shambhala.
30. Whiteley, A. M. and Whiteley, J. (2007). *Core Values and Organizational Change: Theory and Practice*. Hackensack, NJ: World Scientific.
31. Ibid.
32. Kohlrieser, G., IMD Professor George Kohlrieser comments on responsible leadership (January 21, 2009). Retrieved from http://www.imd.org/news/IMD-Professor-George-Kohlrieser-on-responsible-leadership.cfm.
33. Whiteley, A. M. and Whiteley, J. (2007). *Core Values and Organizational Change: Theory and Practice*. Hackensack, NJ: World Scientific.
34. Ames, R. T. and Rosemont, H. (1999). *The Analects of Confucius: A Philosophical Translation*. New York: Ballantine Books.
35. Clemons, S., China's Steve Jobs debate and Deng Xiaoping. *The Atlantic* (November 7, 2011). Retrieved from http://www.theatlantic.com/international/archive/2011/11/chinas-steve-jobs-debate-and-deng-xiaoping/248080.
36. Kohlrieser, G., IMD Professor George Kohlrieser comments on responsible leadership (January 21, 2009). Retrieved from http://www.imd.org/news/IMD-Professor-George-Kohlrieser-on-responsible-leadership.cfm.
37. Zhang, R. (2007). Raising Haier. *Harvard Business Review*, 85(2): 141–146.

Chapter 6

1. Mack, C. S. (2001). *Business Strategy for an Era of Political Change*. Westport, CT Quorum Books.
2. Asan Nanum Foundation, In Asan's words (n.d.). Retrieved from http://www.asan-nanum.org/eng/index/0502.php, URL no longer active.
3. Bellenfant, R., Why Leaders Should Focus on Employee Investment, not Engagement. *Switch & Shift* (October 6, 2014).
4. Bateson, M. C. (2000). *Full Circles, Overlapping Lives: Culture and Generation in Transition*. New York: Random House.
5. Denning, S. (2005). *A Leader's Guide to Storytelling: How to Tell the Right Kind of Story for Every Leadership Challenge*. Chichester: Pfeiffer Wiley.
6. Ibid.
7. Schwass, J., Kralik, M., and Glemser, A.-C. (2013). Hartalega Sdn Bhd (Malaysia). IMD Case IMD-3-2423. Lausanne: IMD.
8. Paddle, I., Masamoto Yashiro explains how Shinsei Bank is getting it right. *FinanceAsia* (November 15, 2005).
9. Soble, J., Toyota's 'ultimate adviser' Eiji Toyoda dies aged 100. *Financial Times* (September 17, 2013).
10. Kelly, T., The outsider. *Forbes* (August 22, 2008).
11. Roll, M. (2006). *Asian Brand Strategy*. Basingstoke: Palgrave Macmillan.

12. Matsushita Institute of Management, Mr. Matsushita's statement (n.d.). Retrieved May 18, 2015, from http://www.mskj.or.jp/english/about_02.html.
13. Vision & Mission. (n.d). Retrieved from http://lkyspp.nus.edu.sg/about-us/vision-and-mission/ Lee Kuan Yew School of Public Policy.
14. Clark, L. (2013). Richard Branson: business can be a force for good. *Wired.* Retrieved, March 22, 2016 from http://www.wired.co.uk/news/archive/2013-06/17/richard-branson-space.
15. Ayala Foundation. Vision Mission Values (2013). Retrieved from http://www.ayalafoundation.org/vision-mission-values/.
16. Whiteley, A. M. and Whiteley, J. (2007). *Core Values and Organizational Change: Theory and Practice.* Hackensack, NJ: World Scientific.
17. Treece, J. B., He put Toyota in the spotlight, but Eiji Toyoda fled the limelight. *Automotive News* (September 23, 2013). Retrieved from http://www.autonews.com/article/20130923/OEM02/309239962/he-put-toyota-in-the-spotlight-but-eiji-toyoda-fled-the-limelight.
18. Tudor, A., Shinsei Bank CEO to retire. *Wall Street Journal* (February 25, 2010). Retrieved from http://www.wsj.com/articles/SB10001424052748703510204575085212958805050.
19. The Japan Prize honors progress in science and technology, and contributions to peace and prosperity.
20. Panasonic, Establishing the PHP Institute: in 1946 at age 51 (n.d.). Retrieved from http://www.panasonic.com/global/corporate/history/konosuke-matsushita/story3-02.html.
21. Ibid.

Chapter 7

1. Lai, A. (2011). Transformational-Transactional Leadership Theory. 2011 AHS Capstone Project, Paper 17, Olin College. Retrieved from http://digitalcommons.olin.edu/cgi/viewcontent.cgi?article=1013&context=ahs_capstone_2011.
2. Bass, B. M. (1990). From transactional to transformational leadership: Learning to share the vision. *Organizational Dynamics*, 18(3): 19–31.
3. Greenleaf, K. R. (1977). *Servant Leadership.* Mahwah, NJ: Paulist Press.
4. Neider, L. L. and Schriesheim, C. A. (2011). The Authentic Leadership Inventory (ALI): Development and empirical tests. *The Leadership Quarterly*, 22(6): 1146–1164.
5. Heifetz, R. A., Linsky, M., and Grashow, A. (2009). *The Practice of Adaptive Leadership: Tools and tactics for changing your organization and the world.* Cambridge, MA: Harvard Business Press.
6. Pearce, C. L., Conger, J. A., and Locke, E. A. (2008). Shared leadership theory. *The Leadership Quarterly*, 19(5): 622–628.
7. Crossan, M. and Mazutis, D. (2008). Transcendent leadership. *Business Horizons*, 51(2): 131–139.
8. Caldwell, C. and Karri, R. (2005). Organizational governance and ethical systems: A covenantal approach to building trust. *Journal of Business Ethics*, 58(1-3): 249–259. doi: 10.1007/s10551-005-1419-2; Hosmer, L. T. (2010). *The Ethics of Management.* McGraw-Hill Higher Education.

9. Pava, M. (2003). *Leading with Meaning: Using covenantal leadership to build a better organization*. New York: Palgrave Macmillan Trade.
10. Flores, R. C. and Flores, F. (2001). *Building Trust: In Business, Politics, Relationships, and Life*. New York: Oxford University Press.
11. Podrug, N., Filipovic, D., and Milic, S. (2010). Critical Overview of Agency Theory. *Annals of DAAAM for 2010 & Proceedings of the 21st International DAAAM Symposiums*, 21(1): 1227–1228.
12. Summary of Literature: Effective Stewardship. (2014). Stewardship Asia Centre & IMD. Singapore. Retrieved from http://www.stewardshipasia.com.sg/knowledge/effective_stewardship.pdf.
13. Kirkpatrick, S. A. and Locke, E. A. (1996). Direct and indirect effects of three core charismatic leadership components on performance and attitudes. *Journal of Applied Psychology*, 81(1): 36–51.
14. CNN (2007). Transcript: Masamoto Yashiro, former chairman & CEO, Shinsei Bank. Retrieved from http://edition.cnn.com/2007/BUSINESS/01/14/boardroom.yashiro.
15. Paddle, I., Masamoto Yashiro explains how Shinsei Bank is getting it right. *FinanceAsia* (November 15, 2005).
16. The Japanese Banker Who Can Say No. *Businessweek International Edition* (October 22, 2000).
17. Crainer, S., Goodness, greatness, Mars. *Business Strategy Review* (July 15, 2014).
18. Malnight, T.W., Keys, T.S., and van der Graaf, K. (2013). *Ready? The 3Rs of Preparing your Organization for the Future*. Rivaz: Strategy Dynamics Global SA.
19. McMahon, T. (2013). Lean Quote: Eiji Toyoda's Respect For People. A Lean Journey. Retrieved from http://www.aleanjourney.com/2013/10/lean-quote-eiji-toyodas-respect-for.html.
20. Freiberg, K., Freiberg, J., and Dunston, D. (2011). *Nanovation: How a Little Car Can Teach the World to Think Big and Act Bold*. Nashville, TN: Thomas Nelson.
21. Q&A with Jaime Augusto Zóbel de Ayala II. (2003). Global Giving Matters.
22. Crainer, S. and Dearlove, D. (2014). Shaping Tomorrow. *Business Strategy Review*, 25(4): 8–13.
23. Schön, D. A. (1983). *The Reflective Practitioner: How Professionals Think in Action*. New York: Basic Books.
24. Argyris, C. and Schon, D.A. (1996). *Organizational Learning: Theory, Method and Practice*. Reading, MA: Addison-Wesley.
25. Anderson, L. (1997). Argyris and Schön's theory on congruence and learning. Retrieved from http://www.scu.edu.au/schools/gcm/ar/arp/argyris.html.
26. Senge, P. (1990). *The Fifth Discipline: The Art and Practice of the Learning Organization*. New York: Bantam Doubleday.
27. Palmisano, S. (2006). The Globally Integrated Enterprise. *Foreign Affairs*, 85(3): 127–136.
28. Quinn, B. (2012). Transcript of Kiichiro Toyoda. Retrieved from https://prezi.com/gcgzh9qn_gwr/kiichiro-toyoda-brian-quinn.

29. Rediff, Ratan Tata's words of inspiration (August 26).) *Rediff News* (August 26, 2008). Retrieved from http://m.rediff.com/money/2008/aug/26sli11.htm.
30. Senge, P. (1990). *The Fifth Discipline: The Art and Practice of the Learning Organization.* New York: Bantam Doubleday.
31. Harvard Business School. (2004). Minoru Makihara, 75th AMP, 1977. *Harvard Alumni Stories.* Retrieved from https://www.alumni.hbs.edu/stories/Pages/story-bulletin.aspx?num=2014.
32. Quinn, B. (2012). Transcript of Kiichiro Toyoda. Retrieved from https://prezi.com/gcgzh9qn_gwr/kiichiro-toyoda-brian-quinn.

Chapter 8

1. Flannery, R., 8 (Genuine!) tips for success from Asia's richest man Li Ka-shing. *Forbes* (March 8, 2012).
2. Deloitte. (2014). Global Risk Survey – Reputation@Risk. Retrieved from http://www2.deloitte.com/global/en/pages/governance-risk-and-compliance/articles/reputation-at-risk.html.
3. The other four firms are PricewaterhouseCoopers, Deloitte Touche Tohmatsu, Ernst & Young, and KPMG.
4. Tuttle, B., Warren Buffett's boring, brilliant wisdom. *Time* (March 1, 2010). Retrieved from http://business.time.com/2010/03/01/warren-buffetts-boring-brilliant-wisdom.
5. Crippen, A., Warren Buffett's 9 rules for running a business. *CNBC* (November 11, 2014). Retrieved from http://www.cnbc.com/id/102156277.
6. Unconscious competence, the fourth stage of competence, relates to the psychological states involved in the process of progressing from incompetence to competence in a skill.
7. Hay Group (n.d.). Executive blind spots. Retrieved from http://www.haygroup.com/us/downloads/details.aspx?id=7347.
8. Chang, H.J. (2000). The hazard of moral hazard: Untangling the Asian crisis. *World Development,* 28(4): 775–788.
9. Anchoring refers to the tendency to base decision-making on the first piece of information received, which may not be relevant to the current decision. Conjunction fallacy is the result of flawed reasoning based on the assumption that specific conditions are more likely than more general ones. Illusory correlation is the false perception of a relationship between events or people (or other variables), which underlies stereotyping, for example.
10. The International Jew: The World's Problem. *The Dearborn Independent* (May 22, 1920). Retrieved from http://www.henryford.fr/critiques/dearborn-independent.
11. The Swatch Group brands include Swatch, Blancpain, Omega, Longines, Rado, Tissot, Certina, Mido, Hamilton, Pierre Balmain, Calvin Klein, Flik Flak, Breguet, and Lanco.
12. Oliver, S. (2015). Swiss watch industry headed for an "ice age" thanks to Apple Watch, Swatch inventor says. Retrieved from http://appleinsider.com/articles/15/03/10/swiss-watch-industry-headed-for-an-ice-age-thanks-to-apple-watch-swatch-inventor-says.

13. Flannery, R., 8 (Genuine!) tips for success from Asia's richest man Li Ka-shing. *Forbes* (March 8, 2012).
14. Quoteswise (n.d.) Li Ka-shing Quotes. Retrieved from http://www. quoteswise.com/li-ka-shing-quotes-2.html.
15. McKeown, L. (2013). Five ways to see your business blind spots. Inc. Retrieved from http://www.inc.com/les-mckeown/5-ways-to-see-your-business-blind-spots.html.
16. Khann, T., Song, J., and Lee, K. (2011). The global paradox of Samsung's rise. *Harvard Business Review*, July–August. Retrieved from https://hbr.org/2011/ 07/the-globe-the-paradox-of-samsungs-rise.
17. Girion, L., GE succession a leadership lesson. *LA Times* (December 3, 2000).
18. Kenney, C. (1991). *Riding the Runaway Horse: The Rise and Decline of Wang Laboratories*. Boston: Little Brown & Co.
19. Zillman, C., With co-CEOs, companies flirt with disaster. *Fortune* (September 20, 2014). Retrieved from http://Fortune.com/2014/09/20/oracle-two-ceos-disaster.
20. Bach, D. and Allen, D.B. (2010). What every CEO needs to know about nonmarket strategy. *MIT Sloan Management Review*, 51(3): 41–48. Retrieved from http://sloanreview.mit.edu/article/what-every-ceo-needs-to-know-about-nonmarket-strategy.

Chapter 9

1. Çelik, S. and Isaksson, M. (2013). Institutional Investors as Owners – Who Are They and What Do They Do? OECD Corporate Governance Working Papers. Retrieved from http://www.oecd-ilibrary.org/governance/institutional-investors-as-owners_5k3v1dvmfk42-en?crawler=true.
2. Towers Watson. (2014). The World's 500 Largest Asset Managers – Year end 2013. Retrieved from http://www.towerswatson.com/en/Insights/IC-Types/ Survey-Research-Results/2014/11/The-worlds-500-largest-asset-managers-year-end-2013.
3. Kohn, A. H. and Yip-Williams, J.L., The Separation of Ownership from Ownership. Director Notes. *The Conference Board* (November 2013). Retrieved from https://www.conference-board.org/retrievefile.cfm?filename=TCB_DN-V5N22-131.pdf&type=subsite.
4. Wong, S., Why Stewardship is Proving Elusive for Institutional Investors. Harvard Law School Forum on Corporate Governance and Financial Regulation (July 31, 2010). Retrieved from http://corpgov.law.harvard.edu/2010/07/31/ why-stewardship-is-proving-elusive-for-institutional-investors.

Appendix A

1. Abrahamson, E. and Hambrick, D. C. (1997). Attentional homogeneity in industries: The effect of discretion. *Journal of Organizational Behavior*, 18(7): 513–532.

2. Carley, K. M. (1997). Extracting team mental models through textual analysis. *Journal of Organizational Behavior*, 18(7): 533–558.

3. Short, J. C., Brigham, K. H., Broberg, J. C. et al. (2009). Family firms and entrepreneurial orientation in publicly traded firms: a comparative analysis of the S&P 500. *Family Business Review*, 22(1): 1-1. doi: 10.1177/0894486508327823.

4. Bowman, E. H. (1984). Word content analysis of annual reports for corporate strategy and risk. *Interfaces*, 14: 61–71.

5. Michalisin, M. D. (2001). Validity of annual report assertions about innovativeness: An empirical investigation. *Journal of Business Research*, 53(3): 151–161.

6. Anthony, L. (n.d.) AntLab: AntConc. Laurence Anthony's website. http://www.laurenceanthony.net/software/antconc/

7. This exercise can be tested by replacing specific companies in the sample by other companies, or expanding the number of annual reports under analysis. Nonetheless, it is useful to keep in mind that stewardship is by definition a long-term phenomenon. Positive word counts are total counts of words specific to our sample of companies potentially ranking high on stewardship. Negative word counts are total counts of words specific to our sample of companies potentially ranking low on stewardship.

8. Larcker, D. F. and Zakolyukina, A. A. (2012). Detecting Deceptive Discussions in Conference Calls. *Journal of Accounting Research*, 50(2): 495–540.

9. 10-K wrap is "a summary report of a company's annual performance that bundles the 10-K report required by the Securities and Exchange Commission (SEC) with additional commentary from the company, covering such things as the corporate vision, letter to shareholders and business overview among other topics. The 10-K wrap is often released instead of a traditional annual report and generally contains fewer images and comments from management." http://www.investopedia.com/terms/1/10k-wrap.asp.

10. Quick Ratio = (Cash & Equivalents + Receivables (Net)) / Total Current Liabilities.

11. Return on Equity: amount of net income returned as a percentage of shareholders' equity. Return on equity measures a corporation's profitability by revealing how much profit a company generates with the money shareholders have invested. http://www.investopedia.com/terms/r/returnonequity.asp.

Index

Compiled by James Helling, INDEXING SPECIALISTS (UK) Ltd., Indexing House, 306A Portland Road, Hove, East Sussex BN3 5LP United Kingdom